TOP LAWYERS
& Their Famous Cases

TOP LAWYERS
& Their Famous Cases

Phyllis Raybin Emert

The Oliver Press, Inc.
Minneapolis

The Oliver Press, Inc.
Charlotte Square
5707 West 36th Street
Minneapolis, MN 55416-2510

For Judy Wolman

The author wishes to thank administrative law judge Laurence T.
Emert, without whose help this book would not have been possible.

The publisher wishes to thank John Satorius of the Fredrikson and
Byron law firm in Minneapolis for his review of this manuscript.

Library of Congress Cataloging-in-Publication Data

Emert, Phyllis Raybin.
Top lawyers and their famous cases / Phyllis Raybin Emert.
p.   cm. — (Profiles)
Includes bibliographical references and index.
ISBN 1-881508-31-5 (library binding)
1. Lawyers—United States—Biography—Juvenile literature. 2.
Trials—United States—Juvenile literature. [1. Lawyers. 2. Trials.]
I. Title. II. Series: Profiles (Minneapolis, Minn.)
KF353.E447   1996
340'.092'273—dc20
[B]   95-42908
                                                                    CIP
                                                                     AC

ISBN: 1-881508-31-5
Profiles XXI
Printed in the United States of America

02 01 00 99 98 97 96   7 6 5 4 3 2 1

Contents

The staff of the Southern Poverty Law Center uses the legal system in the courts to fight for justice and equality for all.

Introduction

*L*awyers have played a critical role in the history of the United States. Outspoken and at times controversial, they have used the law and the courts to wage some of the most significant battles for social, economic, and political change during the past 300 years.

Lawyers advise clients about their legal rights and obligations. They try both civil and criminal cases before judges and juries in which money or an individual's freedom is at stake. They appear before the United States Supreme Court to argue that a law is *unconstitutional*, or not in keeping with the U.S. Constitution. Lawyers also may argue that legal *precedents*, or laws or rulings upon which current laws are based, should be changed because they are wrong or outdated.

While most people respect lawyers for their dedication to the causes of their clients, others criticize them.

Despite these mixed feelings, few Americans could deny the contributions that lawyers have made to their country. Throughout American history, lawyers have played prominent leadership roles. Lawyers drafted the Declaration of Independence and the U.S. Constitution. More than 20 presidents, including Thomas Jefferson, James Madison, William Howard Taft, Calvin Coolidge, Gerald Ford, and Bill Clinton, were lawyers before becoming president.

The founders of the United States considered legal representation so necessary that they wrote the Sixth Amendment to the Constitution. This amendment states that "in all criminal prosecutions, the accused shall enjoy the right . . . to have Assistance of Counsel for his defense."

In the more than 200 years since the drafting of the Constitution and Bill of Rights, preparation for the profession of law has undergone major changes. Lawyers such as John Adams and Abraham Lincoln received their legal training by studying law books or working in law offices. But by the late nineteenth century, lawyers usually had to attend law school and pass a difficult examination to be admitted to practice before the *bar*, or the court.

Top Lawyers and Their Famous Cases introduces eight notable American lawyers. Some are well known; others may be unfamiliar. But all share a commitment to the causes of justice, fairness, and equality, as well as a commitment to the legal needs of the clients they represent.

This book begins in the colonial period with Andrew Hamilton, the foremost lawyer in the American

*Many U.S. presidents
have had legal training
as part of their
education. They
include (right) Thomas
Jefferson (1743-1826),
William Howard Taft
(1857-1930)—who
later became chief
justice of the U.S.
Supreme Court--
and Bill Clinton, the
forty-second president.*

colonies. Without his skillful defense of a newspaper printer, the freedom of the press as we know it today in the United States might not exist.

John Adams and Abraham Lincoln are well known as the second and sixteenth presidents of the United States, respectively, yet both were also well-respected lawyers who had flourishing and distinguished legal careers before becoming president. John Adams's actions in representing the British soldiers involved in the Boston Massacre helped to establish the principle that even unpopular causes (and clients) have a right to legal representation and justice. Lincoln's representation of both ordinary citizens and the powerful railroads helped to prepare him for the challenge of the presidency and the terrible ordeal of the Civil War.

Belva Lockwood practiced law at a time when few women were allowed to be lawyers. Lockwood was the first woman lawyer to appear before the Supreme Court, and her legal skills in representing the Cherokees won them the largest claim on behalf of an American Indian tribe up to that time.

In his passionate defense of a young teacher in *Tennessee v. Scopes*, Clarence Darrow, considered by many to be the greatest American trial lawyer who ever lived, helped to establish the principle of academic freedom and emphasized the need for the separation of church and state. His use of psychiatric testimony in the Leopold-Loeb murder trial in the 1920s was controversial and unprecedented at the time but has since influenced the defense of many individuals.

Associate Justice Robert H. Jackson of the United States Supreme Court was chief U.S. prosecutor at the Nuremberg, Germany, war-crimes trials following World War II. He helped to establish the principle that even in war, individuals will be held responsible for acts that violate international law.

When remaining silent was much safer than speaking out, Joseph Welch, representing the U.S. Army, took on Senator Joseph McCarthy, one of the most powerful political figures of his day, in the Army-McCarthy hearings. Welch successfully used for the first time the medium of television to expose McCarthy to the American people.

As a southern lawyer committed to civil rights, Morris Dees has taken organizations that advocate racial hatred and violence to court, often at great personal risk. In his lawsuit against the Ku Klux Klan, he helped to establish the precedent that groups advocating violence against minorities will be held financially accountable for the actions of their members.

All the lawyers in this book were willing to represent unpopular clients or matters of far-reaching consequence. Some challenged bad laws and ultimately helped to change them. Others risked their lives and careers as they fought for equal justice. All shared a respect for the law and compassion for the people they represented. They exemplify the very best in what many consider to be a truly noble profession, and their impact is still felt today.

Andrew Hamilton (1676?-1741) rose from obscurity to become one of the greatest and most influential lawyers in colonial America.

1

Andrew Hamilton
Freedom to Write the Truth

*T*he city hall courtroom at Nassau and Wall Streets in New York City was packed with spectators on the morning of August 4, 1735. The crowd was there to witness the trial of printer John Peter Zenger.

According to Richard Bradley, attorney general of the colony of New York, Zenger's publication, the *New York Weekly Journal*, contained "false, scandalous, and seditious libel" about the king of England and his governor in New York. Bradley maintained that the newspaper had encouraged *sedition*, or discontent and rebellion against the government, by publishing material that *libeled*, or attacked and injured the reputation of, the king and his governors.

John Chambers, the attorney assigned by the court to defend Zenger, entered a plea of "not guilty." As people pressed forward to hear, Attorney General Bradley delivered his opening statement about the nature of libel. When Bradley had finished, an older, distinguished gentleman left his seat in the crowd and walked forward to face the justices. The crowd gave a collective gasp when the man identified himself as Andrew Hamilton of Philadelphia, one of the best-known and most highly respected attorneys in all the colonies. "May it please your honor," Hamilton said, "I am concerned in this case on the part of Mr. Zenger, the defendant."

Chief Justice James De Lancey, who had already barred Zenger's original lawyers from the court, could not possibly prevent a man of such importance and reputation from representing Zenger. The chief justice allowed Hamilton to participate in what would become one of the most significant trials in American history. When the American colonies became the United States of America following the Revolutionary War, the 1735 trial provided the foundation for establishing the freedom of the press in the United States.

At the time of Zenger's trial, dissatisfaction with British rulers was widespread throughout the colonies. Governors, who were appointed by the king, could veto acts of the state assemblies. These men often were corrupt and greedy tyrants who used the laws to fill their own pockets.

Before coming to New York, William Cosby had governed the British island colony of Minorca. But he had been forced from office for abusing the powers of his position.

One such tyrant was William Cosby, whom the king had appointed as governor of New York in 1731. Cosby spent months traveling in Europe before arriving at his new post in August 1732. In the interim, the president of the king's council, Rip Van Dam, had assumed the position of acting governor and had received the salary and fees of the office.

When Cosby finally arrived in New York, the assembly voted him a salary of 1,500 pounds (the British monetary unit). He was also given an illegal gift of 750 pounds for helping to repeal a sugar bill that the assembly considered harmful to the colonists—and this gift was later raised to 1,000 pounds because Cosby thought the original amount had not been large enough. Cosby also demanded that Rip Van Dam pay him half of the salary and fees he had received as the interim governor. When Van Dam refused, Cosby took him to court.

After Lewis Morris, the chief justice of the New York Supreme Court, ruled against Cosby, the governor retaliated by removing Morris from the court without consulting the council. He then appointed another justice, James De Lancey, to replace Morris as chief justice. Morris had been a distinguished judge, and Cosby's abuse of power stunned and infuriated the New York colonists.

Morris, Van Dam, and other respected colonists formed the Popular Party to oppose Cosby and the Court Party. Since the Court Party controlled New York's only newspaper, the *Gazette*, the leaders of the Popular Party proposed that John Peter Zenger publish an opposition newspaper, the *New York Weekly Journal*. Zenger, a German immigrant who had served as a printer's *apprentice*, or unpaid trainee, agreed. The first issue appeared on November 5, 1733. The four-page paper published anonymous articles written by Popular Party leaders that dealt with such topics as freedom of the press, the obligations of government, and the arbitrary actions of the Cosby administration. Later issues continued to criticize the current government. One article stated that colonists were seeing "men's deeds destroyed, judges arbitrarily displaced, new courts erected without consent of the legislature." Another declared that if the situation did not change, the people of New York would see their liberties and property taken from them, making them slaves.

16

As the Popular Party grew in strength, they ran candidates in the elections of city officials. Following their election victories, two songs celebrating the Popular Party and criticizing the governor were published in the *New York Weekly Journal*.

Through James De Lancey, his appointed chief justice, the infuriated Cosby asked a grand jury to indict John Peter Zenger, the *Journal* publisher, on charges of seditious libel. When the jury refused, the council issued a warrant for Zenger's arrest. The grand jury still refused to indict him. Finally, Richard Bradley, Cosby's attorney general, charged Zenger with printing "false, scandalous, and seditious libel."

After his arrest, Zenger asked for a reasonable bail. He gave his net worth as 40 pounds, but Chief Justice De Lancey set bail at 400 pounds. Because he could not make bail, Zenger remained in jail for more than nine months until the trial was over. During this time, Zenger's wife continued to print the newspaper, including accounts of the trial proceedings.

Zenger's two attorneys, William Smith and James Alexander, were members of the Popular Party. Before the trial began, Smith and Alexander challenged the legality of the two current supreme court justices—De Lancey and Frederick Philipse—on the grounds that the governor had appointed them without seeking the council's approval. De Lancey angrily responded that either he and Philipse "must go from the bench or you from the bar; therefore we exclude you . . . from the bar." After he ordered Smith and Alexander from the courtroom, the

Under Governor Cosby's orders, copies of John Peter Zenger's New York Weekly Journal *were seized and burned.*

two lawyers contacted Andrew Hamilton to take over Zenger's defense.

Under early English common law, the law of libel was based on the doctrine that any criticism of the government was seditious, whether it was true or false, because injury could result from either a true or a false statement. Sir William Blackstone, a noted eighteenth-century British lawyer, wrote in the 1760s that the crime was in the printing of the libel, not in its truth or falsehood. Thus, in the mid-eighteenth century, the crime of libel concerned the publication of comments rather than the facts themselves or why they had been printed. According to one historian, English lawyers often said that "the greater the truth, the greater the libel."

In a trial for seditious libel, the only question the jury was allowed to decide was whether the accused had created a publication. In Zenger's case, this meant the jury could decide only whether he in fact had published the newspaper. The judges would then rule on whether the writing was libelous under the law. Therefore, if the jury found that Zenger had published the *New York Weekly Journal*, Cosby's justices could quickly decide that the newspaper articles were libelous.

This was the situation Andrew Hamilton faced as he stood before the justices on August 4, 1735. Hamilton was nearly 60 years old and ill, but he was still eager to take on the case.

Andrew Hamilton was born in Scotland in the mid-1670s. He had come to America in his early twenties and eventually settled in Kent County, Maryland. There

Hamilton married Anne Preston, a wealthy widow who had valuable political and social connections. After studying law, Hamilton opened a law office and was soon elected to the Maryland Assembly. He finished his law studies at the Inns of Court in London and, in 1712, became a member of the English bar—a prestigious achievement for a colonial American.

Hamilton's growing reputation as a skilled lawyer and his frequent business trips to Philadelphia brought him to the attention of William Penn, the founder of Pennsylvania, who retained him as his personal attorney. Hamilton moved to Philadelphia in 1712. He served as attorney general of the colony of Pennsylvania from 1717 to 1726 and, in 1727, became recorder of the city of Philadelphia. In 1728, Hamilton accepted the position of *prothonotary*, or chief clerk, of the supreme court in Philadelphia. That same year, he was also elected to the colonial assembly from Bucks County, and he became speaker of the assembly in 1729. He was such a respected political figure that governors of the other colonies sought his advice on political and economic matters.

Hamilton was also responsible for designing and building a new Philadelphia state house. After serving as the site of the Continental Congress that met in 1776 to adopt the Declaration of Independence, this building would become known as Independence Hall.

Hamilton knew that if he took the Zenger case, he had a lot to lose. He risked the anger of the British officials and the possibility that they would retaliate against him. But Hamilton strongly believed in the people's right

After being persecuted in England for his Quaker beliefs, William Penn (1644-1718) moved to America and founded the colony of Pennsylvania in 1681.

to criticize their government and to expose any corruption that existed. Therefore, he considered representing Zenger to be a privilege, and he took on his defense *pro bono*, or without charging a fee for his services.

Hamilton planned his legal strategy carefully. Secrecy was important because he wanted to catch his opponents off guard and undermine their confidence. His unexpected appearance in the courtroom was the first surprise of the trial. The second came moments later when the esteemed attorney openly admitted that Zenger had printed the newspapers in question. Seeing this as an opening, Attorney General Bradley (who was acting as prosecutor at the trial) tried to end the trial immediately.

Stepping forward, he argued that Hamilton's admission meant that only one verdict was possible: Zenger was guilty of libel. Hamilton responded by arguing that printing alone did not make the words a libel. "The words themselves must be libelous, that is, false, scandalous, and seditious, or else we are not guilty," he stated.

Bradley pointed out that criticism of the government constituted libel even if the criticism were true. But Hamilton replied that the original indictment against Zenger would not have included the word "false" unless it were intended to have some meaning. "The falsehood makes the scandal, and both make the libel," Hamilton declared. Bradley must prove that what Zenger printed was false. Refusing to respond to Hamilton's challenge, Bradley stated flatly, "We have nothing to prove."

When Hamilton offered to prove that the newspaper statements were true, Chief Justice De Lancey cut him off, declaring that a person could not "justify" a libel. Hamilton offered examples of cases in which the falseness of a libel had affected the court's final decision. But De Lancey refused to allow Hamilton to prove the truth of what Zenger had printed.

When he realized he could make no progress with the judges, Hamilton tried a different strategy. Turning to the jury, Hamilton said they had to decide if the facts Zenger had printed were "false, scandalous, and seditious" or true. De Lancey interrupted, reminding Hamilton that the jury was responsible only for finding out whether Zenger had printed and published the papers. The matter of law would be left to the court.

Hamilton responded by arguing that a jury had the right to determine both the law and the fact of the libel. If the court did not allow the jury to do this, he maintained, then the jury was a useless institution. He also noted that in judging others, the jury members were to make use of their own perceptions and consciences. Hamilton added that if the court and the jury were to accept Bradley's definition of libel, then almost everything that was written could potentially be called libel, and no writer would be safe from being called a libeler.

Hamilton next turned to abuses of power, arguing that citizens had the right to criticize these abuses and to correct them. "Power," he said, "may justly be compared

The crowd in the Zenger trial was riveted to the battle between the celebrity lawyer, Andrew Hamilton (standing with arm raised), and Governor Cosby's political allies.

to a great river." Such a river, "while kept within its bounds, is both beautiful and useful; but when it overflows its banks, it . . . brings destruction and desolation wherever it comes." Thus, Hamilton concluded, we must "support liberty, the only bulwark against lawless power."

Hamilton's eloquent closing comments to the jurors were memorable. He told them they were involved with more than the case of a poor New York City printer. Stressing that the trial affected every free person who lived under British rule, Hamilton pointed out that all people who preferred freedom to slavery would welcome their verdict of "not guilty." The jurors, he declared, had the right and the liberty "of exposing and opposing arbitrary Power . . . by speaking and writing Truth."

Chief Justice De Lancey then reminded the jury that regardless of what Hamilton had said, they should limit their deliberations to the question of publication (which had already been admitted) and leave the question of libel to the court. De Lancey, however, could not control the jury's decision. After withdrawing for only ten minutes, the jurors returned to the courtroom. When the foreman, Thomas Hunt, announced a verdict of "not guilty," cheers filled the room. The excited crowd marched outside and down the street, and John Peter Zenger was released from jail the following day.

That evening, Andrew Hamilton celebrated with 40 well-wishers at the Black Horse Tavern. After being toasted all night, Hamilton raised his glass and shouted, "To the law—may it always prevail!" The next morning, the great guns of several ships in the harbor saluted

Hamilton. The following month, New York City's mayor and council made him an honorary citizen.

The term "Philadelphia lawyer," meaning an exceptionally smart, shrewd, and skillful attorney, came from Hamilton's defense of Zenger. After the Zenger trial, Hamilton returned to the colonial assembly and his law practice in Philadelphia. In 1737, he was appointed judge of the *admiralty court*, which ruled on cases occurring at sea. Two years later, Hamilton retired from the assembly. In a farewell speech before that body, he declared that his chief aim had always been the preservation of liberty. Hamilton died in 1741 around the age of 65.

The Zenger trial established in the American colonies the principles that the jury can decide both the law and the facts in libel cases and that truth is an absolute defense against a charge of libel. Fifty-seven years later, in 1792, the British Libel Act gave English juries the same power to decide whether a statement was libelous.

More than 50 years following the Zenger trial, the framers of the U.S. Constitution drafted a Bill of Rights that included the First Amendment. Hamilton's defense at the Zenger trial had directly influenced the passage of this amendment, which states that "Congress shall make no law . . . abridging the freedom of speech or of the press." It was former chief justice Lewis Morris's grandson, Gouverneur Morris, a member of the Constitutional Convention, who declared that Hamilton's defense at the Zenger trial was "the germ of American freedom—the morning star of that liberty which subsequently revolutionized America."

*John Adams (1735-1826) served as vice-president
(1789-1797) and president (1797-1801) of the
United States in an era when conflicting plans for the
future of the new nation created fierce rivalries.*

2

John Adams
Furthering the Cause of Justice

*B*y 1770, at age 34, John Adams already had a reputation as a renowned lawyer and an outspoken patriot. Unlike his second cousin, Sam Adams, who sometimes supported violence in promoting the cause of liberty, John Adams preferred to use the written and spoken word to persuade opponents to adopt his view of justice and the law.

On March 5, 1770, the event that became known as the Boston Massacre changed the life of John Adams and every other American colonist. That night, several British soldiers, following threats and taunts from an unruly

American mob, had fired into the crowd. When the smoke had cleared, three colonists were dead and eight were wounded, two fatally. Lieutenant Governor Thomas Hutchinson of Massachusetts ordered the arrest of Captain Thomas Preston, the officer in charge, and the eight British soldiers who had fired into the crowd, charging all of them with murder.

Tension ran so high in Boston that the accused British soldiers could not find a lawyer to defend them in court. Attorneys loyal to British king George III refused the case for fear of the mob and the Sons of Liberty. This secret network of militant patriot organizations was formed in 1765 to protest the Stamp Act, the first direct tax imposed on the American colonists. The Sons of Liberty encouraged the destruction of all documents and publications that carried the required stamp as well as violence against British officials.

Three lawyers who were loyal to the king had already refused to defend Captain Preston when James Forester (Forrest in some sources), a custom-house agent, turned to Adams. Forester told him that two other lawyers had agreed to represent Preston and his fellow soldiers, but only if Adams would act with them. Adams declared that lawyers and the courts should "be independent and impartial at all times and in every circumstance" and agreed to defend Captain Preston. He realized that more than his career or the lives of the British soldiers was involved. Also at stake was law and justice—the presumption that a defendant was innocent until proven guilty in a court of law.

Adams faced much hostility in Boston because of his decision to represent the British soldiers and their captain. People jeered at Adams, threw mud at him, and even hurled rocks through the windows of his home. Yet Adams remained determined to respect the law. His perseverance, honesty, and regard for law and order were characteristics that he would exhibit throughout his long and influential life.

John Adams was born in Braintree in the colony of Massachusetts on October 19, 1735. His father was a farmer and shoemaker who served as a town official, a lieutenant in the town militia, and a church officer. John dreamed of becoming a farmer like his father, but his father had different plans for his oldest son. Reluctantly following his father's wishes, John studied hard and gained entrance to Harvard College, while his younger brothers inherited the Adams's farm when they came of age.

At Harvard, Adams studied Latin, Greek, logic, rhetoric, science, moral philosophy, and mathematics. On his own and in school clubs, he also explored literature and history. An excellent student, Adams graduated in 1755 at the age of 19. Rejecting medicine and religion as career choices, he decided to become a lawyer. While supporting himself as a schoolteacher, Adams studied law with James Putnam, an attorney in Worcester, for two years. He became a lawyer on November 6, 1758, and soon opened a practice in Braintree.

As the years passed, Adams's legal skills and his reputation for honesty grew along with his caseload. During these years as a lawyer, he traveled the court circuits throughout Massachusetts, taking on cases and meeting people from all walks of life.

By the time of his marriage in 1764, Adams was becoming well established as a lawyer and a community leader. His move from being a loyal subject of the king to becoming an outspoken patriot of the American cause had begun three years earlier when he heard James Otis and Oxenbridge Thacher argue against the British Writs of Assistance. British officials in the colonies used these writs—which were essentially search warrants—to hunt for smuggled goods anywhere at any time.

With the passage of the Stamp Act, Adams began to take a more active role in the move toward independence.

Lawyer James Otis (1725-1783), one of John Adams's heroes, led the radical resistance to British authority. Always flamboyant and unpredictable, Otis lost his political influence in the late 1760s when he went insane.

To show their opposition to the hated Stamp Act, the colonists terrorized tax collectors and British officials by plundering their homes and offices and tarring and feathering them.

The Stamp Act required that all newspapers, documents, bills, and papers bear a stamp. The money collected by the British government from selling the stamps would be used to pay for colonial defense. The colonists denounced the Stamp Act because they considered it an excessive and unfair tax. In October 1765, delegates from nine colonies met in New York to protest "taxation without representation."

Adams wrote the "Braintree Instructions," arguing that the Stamp Act in its taxation without representation would strip Americans "of our most essential rights and liberties." Late in 1765, he wrote in his diary that the

Stamp Act had made the colonists "more attentive to their Liberties, more inquisitive about them, and more determined to defend them."

Because of colonial resistance, the British Parliament repealed the Stamp Act in March 1766. This victory for the Americans, however, was short-lived. By late 1767, Parliament had passed the Townshend Acts, which imposed new colonial taxes on items such as tea, glass, paper, and paint. After a board of customs commissioners was set up to enforce these laws in the colonies, American merchants began to boycott English goods.

Adams moved to Boston with his wife, Abigail, and their children early in 1768. Soon, several controversial cases would add to his reputation. His first case concerned John Hancock's sailing ship the *Liberty*, which had arrived in Boston's harbor that June, filled with a cargo of fine wines. Most of the wine was unloaded secretly at night to avoid what the colonists considered to be an unfair tax. The next day, when the king's customs agents in Massachusetts came to seize the *Liberty*'s cargo, a riot broke out between a crowd of Americans and a group of sailors from the *Romney*, a British warship that was anchored nearby.

Because the Crown's customs officers feared for their safety, two regiments of British soldiers were stationed in Boston to protect the king's representatives and to keep order. Under their protection, British authorities confiscated the *Liberty*, converting it into a British vessel, and arrested its owner, John Hancock. Hancock—who was the principal financial backer of the Sons of Liberty—

A signature is often called a "John Hancock" because John Hancock (1737-1793) wrote his name first and much larger than any of the other signers of the Declaration of Independence.

asked John Adams to represent him in court. The trial began in November 1768 and went on for months.

The Boston newspapers reported the Hancock case in great detail. Adams argued that the law imposing a duty on imported fine wines was invalid because it had been enacted without the consent of the colonists. "My client . . . never voted for it," Adams said, "and he never voted for any man to make such a law for him."

In England, the consent of the English people was required for a bill to become law. Parliament had declared that the consent of the colonists was presumed. Adams, however, contended that Parliament had no right to assume that the colonists agreed with all of its acts.

The prosecution for the English Crown based its case on a tax enacted by Parliament in 1765 that had required a payment of seven pounds per cask on wines imported from the Portuguese Madeira Islands. Adams challenged the legality of the tax itself and also pointed out that the Crown had denied Hancock the traditional right to a jury trial—a right not respected in the admiralty courts. Although the advocate general for the Crown called dozens of Bostonians to testify, no one spoke out against John Hancock. Because the colonists viewed the law—and the court—as illegal, they felt no need to tell the truth. In fact, witness after witness *perjured* himself, or lied while under oath. Finally, after months of testimony, the Crown dropped the case in March 1769. Adams had won, and Hancock went free. The jubilance of the people over Adams's victory in court was tempered, however, by the presence of British troops everywhere in the city.

Not long after the Hancock case had ended, John Adams became involved in another matter that once again thrust him into the political spotlight. This case involved the Royal Navy's practice of *impressment*—the kidnapping of American men and forcing them into naval service.

On April 22, 1769, the British warship *Rose* was cruising off Marblehead, Massachusetts, looking for new sailors to add to its crew. The *Rose*, commanded by Lieutenant Henry Gibson Panton, stopped a smaller boat, the *Pitt*, which was sailed by a crew of Irish-American immigrants returning to the colonies from Europe with a cargo of salt.

Lieutenant Panton and his men boarded the *Pitt* and selected four sailors for impressment. Armed with knives and harpoons, the sailors barricaded themselves in the hold and warned Panton that they would not be taken into British service. Panton then ordered his men to break the bulkhead. In the struggle that followed, one of the sailors, Michael Corbet, stabbed Panton in the neck with a harpoon, killing him within seconds. British officials immediately arrested the four sailors and charged them with murder on the high seas.

The case was heard in Boston before the admiralty court that had tried John Hancock. In arguing the case for the defense, Adams first moved to obtain a jury trial for the sailors, as he had done in the Hancock trial. When the judges blocked his plea, Adams argued that the killing was justifiable homicide and, thus, no crime had been committed.

The next morning, the court pronounced the judgment. The unanimous decision was that the killing of Lieutenant Panton was indeed justifiable homicide because the sailors had acted in self-defense. This verdict represented Adams's second major successful legal defense against the Crown within the year.

As the months of 1769 passed, tension increased between the people of Boston and the British troops that had been brought in after the riot over the cargo on John Hancock's *Liberty*. Adams wrote a list of grievances for the Massachusetts legislature, declaring that "common decency as well as the honor and dignity of a free legislature demands that the offensive guards be removed from our city." He also called for an inquiry into the offenses of the British soldiers against the people of Boston.

Increasingly militant, the Sons of Liberty and other colonists in Boston who resented the British put pressure on colonial merchants who were not boycotting English goods. To expose them, they put up signs of a painted head mounted on a post. On the morning of February 22, 1770, Ebenezer Richardson, a colonist who was an informer for the customs service, picked up an ax and angrily chopped down one of these signs.

Richardson taunted the mob that had gathered as he struck down the sign, and they began pelting him with stones and snowballs. When Richardson ran inside his house, the mob started throwing stones and bricks at the windows. Frightened, Richardson grabbed his musket and fired into the mob, killing a 12-year-old boy. The angry crowd dragged Richardson to the courthouse and accused him of murder. (He was found guilty a month later but was pardoned by the king.)

Now that the conflict had claimed a victim, confrontations became more frequent and more violent. The killings that became known as the Boston Massacre occurred on March 5, 1770. Risking his career and his personal safety, John Adams agreed to represent Captain Preston and the British soldiers who had fired on the estimated 400 colonists who were threatening them. In making this decision, Adams placed the law and the right to a fair trial above his popularity and personal security.

Although Samuel Adams and the Sons of Liberty wanted an immediate trial, Lieutenant Governor Thomas Hutchinson succeeded in delaying it for seven months. As

The patriots claimed that the victims of the Boston Massacre were martyrs for their cause. They were given a grand funeral, and their deeds were memorialized in widely circulated pamphlets.

time passed, the people of Boston, though unhappy that Adams was representing the British soldiers, still showed respect for him. In fact, much to Adams's surprise, they elected him to fill a vacancy in the Massachusetts legislature while awaiting the start of the trial.

The trial of Captain Thomas Preston for giving the order to fire upon a crowd lasted for five days in late October 1770. Because this was a capital crime, Preston would face execution if he were convicted.

The expert questioning of the prosecution's witnesses by Adams and the other lawyers for the defense— Josiah Quincy, Robert Auchmuty, and Sampson Blowers—revealed contradictions and vague, muddled

John Adams considered his more radical cousin Samuel Adams (1722-1803), the leader of the Sons of Liberty, to be the greatest man of his time.

testimony that cast doubt as to whether Preston had ever given the order to fire. Adams also attempted to show that the Boston crowd had provoked the soldiers into acting in self-defense. If the soldiers had the right to defend themselves under the law, whether or not Preston had given the order to fire was unimportant. Because Adams did not want the enemies of liberty to use the incident to discredit the patriots, he tried to prove Preston's innocence on strictly legal grounds. In fact, he did not even mention Boston's frequent mobs and instead blamed tensions on the British. The Crown's decision to keep a standing army on American soil following the *Liberty* incident had resulted in this violence, Adams declared.

After only a few hours of deliberation, the jury found Preston "not guilty." The acquittal was a legal triumph for John Adams and his colleagues, but their victory was short-lived. An article in the *Gazette* proclaiming "Whoso sheddeth Man's blood, by Man shall his Blood be shed!" brought the temper of the Boston patriots to a boiling point, and some began to plot their revenge.

Four weeks passed between the end of Preston's trial and the beginning of the trial of the eight soldiers. Because Adams believed that jurors from Boston would be more likely to convict the soldiers, he challenged 30 prospective jurors from the city. The judge dismissed these men, and the 12 men who were finally selected lived outside of Boston.

On November 27, 1770, Adams, Josiah Quincy, and Sampson Blowers attempted to prove that the soldiers were innocent of murder. But Adams once again tried to avoid making Bostonians totally responsible for the incident. In his opening statement, Josiah Quincy faced this issue head on by insisting that Bostonians could not be held accountable for the "unjustifiable conduct" of a mob that had gathered in the streets.

The defense called 51 witnesses to the stand. One by one, they painted a picture of an unruly mob of perhaps 400 people who had surrounded the 8 soldiers and threatened to kill them. One witness was Nathaniel Russell, who said, "I saw a number of men and boys armed with clubs and 15 or 20 more coming along, some were damning the soldiers, that they would destroy them, and sink them."

Dr. John Jeffries, surgeon to a colonist named Patrick Carr who had died from wounds suffered on March 5, stated that Carr told him he had "never seen [soldiers] bear half so much before they fired in his life." Carr believed that the man who had shot him "had no malice, but fired to defend himself" and "he forgave the man, whoever he was, that shot him."

Adams's brilliant two-day summation revealed his awareness of the potential personal and political risks for him in taking this case. He declared that if he could save only one life, the blessings and tears of that one person would be, for him, a "sufficient consolation" for "the contempt of mankind."

Adams asked the jury to put themselves in the shoes of the soldiers and to consider the prejudices against them in Boston. Remember, he said, they "had no friends about them" and the people in the crowd were crying, "Kill them! Kill them! Knock them over!" and "heaving snow balls, oyster shells, clubs, white birch sticks three inches and a half diameter." Adams implored, "Consider yourselves in this situation and then judge whether a reasonable man in the soldiers' situation would not have concluded that they were going to kill him."

Adams was careful to distinguish between the law's definitions of murder and of manslaughter. Killing without any provocation was murder, but killing after being provoked by an assault was manslaughter. "Every snow ball, oyster shell, cake of ice or bit of cinder thrown that night at the sentinel and the party of soldiers was an assault upon them," explained Adams. Furthermore, he concluded, "If an assault was made to endanger their lives, the law is clear; they had a right to kill in their own defense. The law will not bend to the uncertain wishes, imaginations and wanton tempers of men."

The jury withdrew for two and one-half hours. When they returned with their verdict, they had found six of the soldiers—William Wemms, James Hartegan, William M'Cauley, Hugh White, William Warren, and John Carrol—"not guilty," and Matthew Killroy and Hugh Montgomery "guilty" of manslaughter, not murder. For the two, Adams asked for "benefit of clergy," which meant they would be branded on the thumb instead of serving jail time. After the two were branded, the court dismissed all of the prisoners.

Although the verdict was not a popular one among the colonists, John Adams later wrote that his defense of Captain Preston and the eight British soldiers was "one of the best Pieces of Service" he ever rendered his country because he had made sure that the law, not the mob, ruled in the colonies.

John Adams would become one of the most important political leaders of his day. He played a key role in the appointment of George Washington as commander-in-chief of the American forces in the Revolutionary War and was a member of the First and Second Continental Congresses, which functioned as the federal legislature of

On July 4, 1776, delegates to the Second Continental Congress signed the Declaration of Independence, which had been written by lawyer and statesman Thomas Jefferson after John Adams had declined the task.

the colonies and the new nation. Adams also served on the congressional committee that drafted the Declaration of Independence. In 1783, Adams helped to negotiate the Treaty of Paris that ended the American Revolution. After the war, he served as ambassador to Great Britain from 1785 to 1788.

Following his return to the United States, Adams became the nation's first vice-president under President George Washington. In his single term as the country's second president, Adams used his diplomatic skills to avoid a war with France. When he left office in 1801, the foundation for a strong national government was solidly in place. Adams died on July 4, 1826, the nation's fiftieth birthday, at age 90.

In the Boston Massacre case, John Adams had placed his own career, popularity, and safety at risk to represent unpopular clients and an unpopular cause. He demonstrated that everyone had the right to counsel—a right later guaranteed by the Sixth Amendment to the U.S. Constitution—and that this right was essential in a free and democratic society.

From 1834, when he became an Illinois state legislator, until his election as president of the United States in 1860, Abraham Lincoln (1809-1865) pursued careers in both law and politics.

3

Abraham Lincoln
Honesty, Fairness, and an Equal Chance for All

*I*n the autumn of 1857, Hannah Armstrong's 24-year-old son Duff was arrested for murder. A man had died following a drunken brawl with Duff and another man at a makeshift saloon that had been set up a mile from a religious revival meeting. This saloon drew both local rowdies and Christians from the revival. Coming so soon after her husband's death, Duff's arrest was particularly devastating for his mother. Hannah, however, received a letter from an old family friend that offered a glimmer of hope for her son's future:

Springfield, Ill.
September 18, 1857

Dear Mrs. Armstrong,

I have just heard of your deep affliction, and the arrest of your son for murder. I can hardly believe that he can be capable of the crime alleged against him. It does not seem possible. I am anxious that he be given a fair trial at any rate; and the gratitude for your long continued kindness to me in adverse circumstances prompts me to offer my humble service gratuitously in his behalf.

It will afford me an opportunity to requite in a small degree the favors I received at your hand, and that of your late lamented husband, when your roof afforded me a grateful shelter, without money and without price.

Yours truly,

A. Lincoln

Abraham Lincoln was one of the best lawyers in Illinois, and he was also a well-known political figure. The attributes that accounted for his success in law and in politics—honesty, fairness, and loyalty—led him to set everything else aside and to concentrate on the defense of an old friend in need.

Some 26 years had passed since the 22-year-old Lincoln had come to New Salem, Illinois, in 1831 as a homeless and penniless stranger. Hannah and Jack Armstrong had befriended him and made him part of their family. While Hannah sewed his clothes and cooked for him, Abe played with the children and rocked Duff's

46

cradle. After he left New Salem for Springfield, Illinois, in the spring of 1837 to begin his law practice, Lincoln always remembered the love and kindness the Armstrongs had shown him.

Abraham Lincoln was born on February 12, 1809, in a log cabin in Hardin County, Kentucky. The family, always poor, moved to Indiana when Abe was seven. Two years later, his mother, Nancy Hanks Lincoln, died, and, the following year, Thomas Lincoln married Sarah Bush Johnston, a widow with three children. She was loving and supportive and encouraged Abraham to learn. Young Abe read everything he could get his hands on—the Bible, *Aesop's Fables, Pilgrim's Progress, Robinson Crusoe.* He studied history and biographies and learned about politics and current events.

Fascinated by legal arguments, Abe would walk for miles to observe lawyers from the area battle in the courtroom. Because he was so well informed, people would gather to hear him debate political issues and philosophical ideas or to just tell jokes or funny stories.

In 1830, the Lincoln family moved to Macon County, Illinois, near Decatur. Soon afterwards, Lincoln went to New Salem, where he met and sometimes lived with the Armstrongs. While working to support himself over the next few years—as a farm hand, grocery clerk, postmaster, and surveyor—he attended local trials as often as possible.

In 1832, Lincoln was elected captain of his company of militiamen during the Black Hawk War—fought by white settlers against the Sac and Fox Indian tribes in

Illinois—but he did not take part in any battles. That same year, Lincoln also ran for the state legislature, representing Sangamon County. Although he lost the election, he gained valuable experience in public speaking. Lincoln ran again for the state legislature in 1834. This time, he won his seat, and he was later reelected to three more terms.

At fellow legislator John Todd Stuart's urging, Lincoln decided to become a lawyer. He read and reread Blackstone's *Commentaries on the Laws of England* and learned how to draw up legal documents such as deeds, mortgages, leases, contracts, and bills of sale. Because he was not licensed to practice law, he offered his services to friends and neighbors free of charge.

After reading the basic law texts that were required for becoming a practicing attorney, Lincoln was formally licensed as a lawyer on March 1, 1837, by the state of Illinois. At the time, all that was necessary for admission to the Illinois bar was a certificate from the county court stating that the applicant was of good moral character.

Lincoln's next move was to Springfield, the new state capital, where he became a lawyer in the law office of John Todd Stuart. Much like John Adams had done 75 years before, Lincoln began to travel "the circuit," spending half the year taking cases in the small backwoods county courts that made up the Illinois Eighth Circuit Court. He enjoyed working with rural people and would charge his poverty-stricken clients only what they could afford, often returning a portion of his fees if he thought he had been overpaid. When he was not riding the circuit or attending a session of the state legislature, Lincoln would handle cases at the Springfield law office.

In 1841, Lincoln formed a new law partnership with Stephen T. Logan. Logan helped Lincoln develop into a well-rounded attorney who became increasingly skillful at presenting cases to juries and organizing and preparing legal arguments. Their association ended in 1844 when Logan took on his son as a law partner. Later that year when Lincoln opened his own law office, he asked 25-year-old William H. Herndon to be his new partner.

After 12 years in the Illinois legislature, 37-year-old Lincoln was elected to the U.S. House of Representatives in 1846 as a member of the Whig Party. He moved to

When Lincoln's law partner, William H. Herndon, complained about Lincoln's habit of reading aloud, Lincoln explained, "When I read aloud, two senses catch the idea; first I see what I read; second, I hear it, and therefore I can remember it better."

Washington, D.C., with his wife, Mary, whom he had married in 1842, and sons Robert and Eddie. Unlike many of his constituents, Lincoln opposed the Mexican War, which had begun on May 13, 1846. He also spoke out against the spread of slavery in the new territories that had been gained in the Mexican War.

After losing his bid for reelection in 1848, Lincoln returned to Springfield. Deciding to give his full attention to his law practice, he again rode the Eighth Circuit, spending nearly half the year traveling from one county court to another. Lincoln and Herndon's practice was extremely successful, and they took on more than 100 cases a year. Lincoln was one of the most popular lawyers in the state, famous for his adept handling of juries in cases ranging from murder to land disputes to corporate law. In addition to his skills as a lawyer, Lincoln was respected for his honesty.

During the 1850s, the bulk of Lincoln's practice consisted of civil suits, for which he collected fees ranging from three dollars (from individuals) to thousands of dollars (from large railroad corporations). In the mid-1850s, Lincoln fought the first of his significant cases for the Illinois Central Railroad, *Illinois Central Railroad v. McLean County*. In 1850, the state of Illinois had acquired more than two and one-half million acres of public lands from the federal government for use in the construction of a railroad, which the state legislature had signed over to the Illinois Central Railroad.

As a further inducement to undertake and complete the project, the state exempted the railroad from all state taxes on its property. In place of the property taxes, the state would receive five percent of the railroad's annual gross income for the first six years and seven percent thereafter.

The first section of the railroad was completed during May 1853 in McLean County. Within months, county officials assessed a tax on the railroad's property, claiming the state did not have the power to exempt the railroad from paying county taxes. If McLean County were successful in collecting taxes from the railroad, then, in spite of the state's agreement with the railroad, every other county through which the railroad passed would be entitled to taxes as well.

The case was a battle for power between the state and the counties. Lincoln first offered his services to McLean County. When county officials failed to reply, he wrote to the railroad. Within four days, the Illinois Central had responded with a $250 retainer.

When Lincoln and the railroad lost *Illinois Central Railroad v. McLean County* in the McLean Circuit Court, Lincoln immediately appealed the case to the Illinois Supreme Court. Lincoln's two former partners, John Todd Stuart and Stephen Logan, represented the county. On a second hearing of the case in December 1855, Chief Justice Walter B. Scates of the Illinois Supreme Court accepted Lincoln's argument that it was constitutional for the legislature to exempt the railroad from all taxes, including county taxes, and to replace the tax with a fixed percentage of the taxpayer's earnings. Such an alternative tax was crucial in this case because the railroad would have no money to pay the taxes until the tracks had been completed. The court's ruling saved the Illinois Central Railroad thousands of dollars that it might have had to pay in county taxes.

When Lincoln presented his bill for $2,000 to the railroad, the company refused to pay, claiming it was too high. Lincoln was shocked and furious because he had saved Illinois Central thousands of dollars and removed an obstacle to building the railroad that otherwise could have become a problem in every other county in the state. After consulting six prominent Illinois colleagues, Lincoln increased his demand to $5,000 and took Illinois Central to court. In June 1857, the case went to trial. Lincoln argued that the difficulty of the case and the amount of work he had done, as well as the amount of money he had saved the railroad, made his fee a reasonable one. Lincoln also read statements from his six colleagues confirming that his services were worth $5,000. Within minutes, the jury awarded Lincoln his fee. To collect it, however, Lincoln had to ask the county sheriff to seize Illinois Central property.

Although the legal case had little to do with national politics, *Illinois Central Railroad v. McLean County* was significant to Lincoln's political career because it funded his next campaign. As the national debate over slavery intensified in the 1850s, Lincoln began speaking out against the policies of longtime rival, Senator Stephen A. Douglas, positioning himself to oppose Douglas in the future. With the Illinois Central money, Lincoln decided to run for the Senate against Douglas in 1858 as a Republican.

The seven debates between Lincoln and Democrat Stephen A. Douglas (1813-1861) during the 1858 campaign for the U.S. Senate made Lincoln nationally famous.

Douglas's proposal for "popular sovereignty"—allowing new states to decide whether to permit slavery—disturbed Lincoln, who wanted to limit the spread of a practice he considered to be evil. Although he lost the election to Douglas, his famous debates with his opponent during that campaign thrust Lincoln into national prominence and, ultimately, into the presidency.

Lincoln had more lawyering to do, however, before returning to politics. Again, he represented what he saw as the nation's future—railroads. In the 1850s, midwestern river and rail companies were in intense competition for trade and economic supremacy in the rapidly growing West. A rivalry also existed between the city of Chicago, which depended upon rail transportation, and St. Louis,

Missouri, the premier river city. Into this controversy stepped Abraham Lincoln, who again represented railroad interests in the most celebrated case of his career: *Hurd v. The Rock Island Bridge Company*, also known as the *Effie Afton* case.

The Rock Island Bridge—a drawbridge connecting Rock Island, Illinois, and Davenport, Iowa—was the first railway bridge over the Mississippi River. From the beginning, river transport companies in St. Louis opposed the building of any bridge because they had enjoyed what amounted to a monopoly on commerce with the West. Not wanting to risk losing their economic dominance, St. Louis steamboat and water transportation companies argued that a bridge would obstruct free travel and be a danger to navigation. Despite these protests, the bridge was completed, and the first train passed over the Mississippi River in April 1856.

Because the rivalry was still strong, it would only be a matter of time before a major legal confrontation developed between the river interests and the railroad. The test case came after a May 6, 1856, accident in which the 230-foot-long steamboat *Effie Afton* struck one of the pillars of the new bridge and then catapulted against another pillar as it began to go under the drawbridge. The boat caught fire when a stove overturned, which also ignited the bridge. Although the hated bridge was only damaged—and was quickly rebuilt—riverboat workers rang bells and blew whistles to celebrate its burning.

Owners of the *Effie Afton* sued The Rock Island Bridge Company for damages in the amount of $50,000.

They claimed the river currents created by the pillars had forcibly driven the steamboat into the pillar, making the bridge an "unlawful obstruction to navigation."

Lincoln spent many months preparing for his presentation in court. He interviewed mechanical engineers, and he examined whether the bridge interfered with river traffic and studied the river currents and their effects on navigation. By the time the trial began in September 1857, Lincoln had a nearly encyclopedic knowledge of every technical aspect of the case.

Lincoln's defense was based on two main points: that the accident had occurred through the negligence of the river pilot of the *Effie Afton*, and that people have a right to choose their means of transportation.

For two weeks, Lincoln questioned engineers, pilots, river workers, and eyewitnesses on the stand about river currents and the bridge. In his closing argument, Lincoln spent two days building his case for the railroad, point by point. John J. Duff, a biographer of Lincoln, called Lincoln's defense "his finest hour as a lawyer."

Lincoln argued that the river was like a highway. Every person had a right to cross or pass along it, and no one had the power to limit the way in which it was crossed. After establishing this theoretical right, he described how the nation's growing economy and western settlement depended upon the expansion of the railroads. Lincoln next pointed out that the Rock Island Bridge was of great importance to this growth. "From September 8, 1856, to August 8, 1857, 12,586 freight cars and 74,179 passengers passed over this bridge," he stated.

Lincoln went on to show that with reasonable skill and care, it was not difficult to navigate under the bridge. His technical discussions of river currents demonstrated that the currents had not driven the boat into the pillar. Furthermore, another steamboat, the *Carson*, had traveled without incident under the bridge right before the *Effie Afton* had hit the pillar. He summed up his argument by saying the *Effie Afton* had entered "so far wrong that she never got right" and then asked if the railroad bridge should be blamed for the *Effie Afton*'s errors.

After hours of deliberation, the jurors were unable to agree on a verdict. Nine favored Lincoln and the railroad, while the remaining three opposed them. The judge dismissed the jury, but Lincoln's presentation and the inability of the jury to come to a unanimous decision was considered a victory for rail interests everywhere. (Not until 1862, when Lincoln was president, did the United States Supreme Court finally rule in the railroad's favor.) In addition, daily newspaper coverage of the trial throughout the country added to Lincoln's growing reputation as a skilled attorney.

Following the *Effie Afton* case, Lincoln began preparing for the Duff Armstrong trial, the most celebrated of his several murder cases. This trial is famous among Lincoln admirers because it demonstrated both his loyalty and, in the cross-examination of the prosecution's star witness, his quick wit and resourcefulness.

On August 29, 1857, outside a tavern about a mile from a revival meeting near Virgin's Grove in Illinois, a fight broke out between Duff Armstrong, James Norris,

The neat office depicted in Frank Leslie's Weekly *in the 1850s reportedly bore little resemblance to the actual cramped and messy offices of Lincoln and William H. Herndon.*

and James Metzker. Norris hit Metzker on the back of the head with a club, and Armstrong reportedly hit him in the forehead with a shot from a slingshot. Metzker got on his horse with difficulty and left the scene, falling off several times on his way home. Three days later, Metzker was dead, apparently from blows he had sustained in his fights with Armstrong and Norris. Soon after, the authorities arrested both men, charging them with murder.

Jim Norris was put on trial first. While it was known that he had assaulted Metzker, it was not certain that his blows had caused Metzker's death. The jury convicted Norris of manslaughter, and the judge sentenced him to eight years in the state penitentiary.

Popular opinion ran so high against the two men in Macon County that Armstrong's local attorneys moved for a change of venue, claiming their client could not receive a fair trial there. The judge granted the motion, and the trial was moved to Beardstown, the county seat of nearby Cass County.

Lincoln studied the testimony from the Norris trial and knew the prosecution's star witness was a man named Charles Allen. Allen swore that he had seen Armstrong and Norris hit Metzker—Armstrong in the forehead with a shot from a slingshot and Norris on the back of the head with a club. As the prosecution's only eyewitness, Allen's testimony was crucial.

Lincoln arrived in Beardstown on May 6, 1858, the evening before the trial began. He made sure the jury included younger men who would more easily identify with Duff Armstrong. After Lincoln had cross-examined a number of witnesses, Charles Allen took the stand. He repeated essentially the same story that he had told at the Norris trial: Armstrong had hit Metzker in the forehead with a shot from a slingshot.

Lincoln began his cross-examination by asking Allen to go over the events of the evening of August 29 in detail. Allen testified that he had been standing 150 feet from Metzker and the two men who were fighting with him. Although it was 11 P.M. at night, Allen swore he could see quite clearly because the moon was bright and high in the sky. He then described the slingshot. Again and again, Allen insisted that he could see clearly because of the moonlight and that he remembered the events accurately.

After the witness had completed his account, Lincoln confronted him with an almanac. According to the almanac, at 11 P.M. on August 29, 1857, the moon was not full but barely past the first quarter. Instead of being high in the sky, by 11 P.M. it had nearly disappeared, so there was no way Allen could have seen what he said he had seen. Lincoln had all but destroyed the prosecution's star witness.

Lincoln then called additional witnesses for the defense. Some had seen Metzker fall off his horse. A doctor testified that either the fall from the horse or the blow to the back of the head by Norris could have caused the fatal injury. Finally, a man named Watkins revealed that the slingshot actually belonged to him and that it had never been in Duff Armstrong's possession. Watkins claimed he had thrown his slingshot away in the very spot where it had been found following the incident.

In his closing argument, the prosecutor asked for the death penalty for Armstrong's "atrocious crime." When it was the defense's turn to speak, Lincoln slowly rose to address the jury. He began by questioning Charles Allen's credibility, explaining that the almanac clearly proved the moon could not have shed enough light on the night of the incident for the state's star witness to have observed the encounter in question. And if Allen were mistaken about the moon, Lincoln suggested, he was no doubt in error about other details as well. Lincoln further argued that Metzker's death was more than likely caused by Norris's blow or by the fall from the horse.

After covering the facts of the case, the popular and respected lawyer described his long friendship with the Armstrong family. According to the prosecuting attorney,

In 1863, President Lincoln again helped the Armstrongs when he secured a discharge from the Union army for Duff, who lay ill in a Kentucky hospital.

J. Henry Shaw, Lincoln had tears in his eyes as he spoke and "the sight of his tall, quivering frame, and the particulars of the story he so pathetically told, moved the jury to tears." The jurors "forgot the guilt of the defendant in their admiration of the advocate," and found Duff Armstrong "not guilty" in less than an hour.

When Hannah offered to pay Lincoln, he refused to take a cent, telling her, "Anything I can do for you I will do for you willingly and freely without charges."

In his 23 years as an attorney, Lincoln argued 178 cases before the Illinois Supreme Court, more than any of his contemporaries. He also tried hundreds of cases in the U.S. circuit and district courts. Lincoln was a commanding presence in the courtroom, using common sense and reason in his arguments as well as being capable of great eloquence. People responded to his simple honesty, his sense of fairness, and his powerful presence.

In 1861, Lincoln left his law practice to become the sixteenth president of the United States. His election

The Lincolns with sons (left to right) Willie, Robert, and Tad in 1861. Their young son Eddie had died in 1850. The president fell into a deep depression after Willie died in 1862, and Mary Lincoln suffered a breakdown from which she never fully recovered.

with a minority of the popular vote—his opponents had split the vote three ways—led to the *secession*, or withdrawal, of eleven southern states from the Union, the formation of the Confederacy, and, in 1861, the outbreak of the Civil War.

The war raised legal questions about the power of the president and the federal government over the states. While he was cautious at first, Lincoln asserted the powers of his office and those of the federal government more and more. On January 1, 1863, less than two years after the start of the Civil War, Lincoln issued the Emancipation Proclamation, which declared that all slaves living in the Confederacy were to be free.

Lincoln was assassinated on April 14, 1865, five days after the surrender of Confederate general Robert E. Lee had ended the Civil War. His killer, John Wilkes Booth, an ardent Confederate sympathizer, shot Lincoln while the president was watching a play at Ford's Theater in Washington, D.C. Although Lincoln had lived to see the end of the Civil War, he died before he could implement his plans for rebuilding the South.

While many U.S. presidents have been lawyers, Lincoln's legal experience was crucial to his presidency. One of his biographers, Albert Woldman, argues that "without his twenty-three years of experience at the bar, he might never have become President of the United States." Abraham Lincoln's legal expertise helped him to deal with the constitutional crises brought about by southern secession and the Civil War. Thus, he was able to lead the nation to a successful, though bloody, reunion

On November 19, 1863, in his Gettysburg Address, Lincoln called for "a new birth of freedom" so that "government of the people, by the people, for the people, shall not perish from the earth."

of the states and the ultimate abolition of slavery. In his short but memorable speech to dedicate the military cemetery at Gettysburg, Pennsylvania, Lincoln had expressed the high cost of preserving the nation and living up to the ideals of freedom.

Belva Lockwood (1830-1917) had to fight for admission to law school because she was a woman.

4

Belva Lockwood
Opening Doors

*I*t was not surprising that in 1891 the Cherokees of the eastern United States turned to attorney Belva Lockwood for help in collecting their long-standing monetary claim against the United States government. At 61, Lockwood was a talented lawyer who specialized in pensions, bounties, and land claims. But she was best known for being an outspoken advocate of women's rights and world peace. During her lifetime, Lockwood created opportunities for women and minorities where none had previously existed. Once she described her life by saying "I have never stopped fighting."

The case of the *Eastern and Emigrant Cherokees v. United States* would be one of the most important of Lockwood's career. Representing 15,000 Cherokees, Lockwood studied the history of the claim that dated back to the 1835 Treaty of New Echota. She traveled frequently to North Carolina to interview and collect sworn statements from the thousands of descendants of the original Cherokees affected by the treaty.

In addition to all of her work on the Cherokee case, Lockwood handled other legal cases and attended peace conferences in Italy and Switzerland during this time. She also joined with other women in writing a "Married Woman's Property Bill" that was passed by Congress in June 1896.

Belva Ann Bennett was born in Royalton in western New York on October 24, 1830. Intelligent and outgoing, she enjoyed school. After graduating from the eighth grade, Belva wanted to continue her education at the Royalton Girls' Academy. Although her mother supported Belva's desire for more education, her father, like many people of the day, believed that girls who were too educated would become "old maids."

Undaunted, Belva got a job teaching summer school at her grade school for $5 a week. By September, she had saved enough money to pay for one year's tuition at the Girls' Academy. During the school year, she supported herself with part-time housekeeping jobs, and each summer she returned to teach at her former school.

After graduating from the Girls' Academy, Belva married Uriah McNall on November 8, 1848, and they moved to nearby Gasport, New York. There Belva worked at her husband's sawmill and occasionally wrote poetry and articles. When her husband died in April 1853, two years after a debilitating sawmill accident, Belva was left a widow with a baby daughter. She applied for a teaching position at Royalton, but she turned down the job when she found out that her salary would only be half that of the male teachers.

Observing that most successful people had a college degree, Belva realized that if she and other women wanted to succeed, they would have to find entry into the country's colleges. While her mother cared for her small daughter, Belva brushed up her skills at the Gasport Academy and then attended Genesee Wesleyan Seminary in Lima, New York. Later, she transferred to Genesee College (now Syracuse University). After graduating with honors in three years, Belva became principal at the Lockport Union High School in western New York. Once she was settled, her daughter rejoined her and became a student at the school. Despite the vocal opposition of some parents, Belva introduced nature walks, physical education, and public speaking for Lockport's female students. Tired of continuing opposition to her innovative curriculum, she opened her own school for girls in Owego, New York, in 1863.

After the end of the Civil War, Belva McNall and her daughter moved to Washington, D.C., where she taught for a year before opening one of the city's first private schools for boys and girls. Belva's struggle to expand education for girls inspired her to take a more

Elizabeth Cady Stanton (1815-1902) helped to organize the 1848 women's rights convention at Seneca Falls, New York. Her "Declaration of Sentiments" for women's rights, which was modeled after the Declaration of Independence, influenced Susan B. Anthony (1820-1906), who along with Stanton (left) led the women's suffrage movement in the nineteenth century.

active role in the women's movement. Whenever she had the time, Belva would attend sessions of Congress and the Supreme Court. She also began suffrage work to bring the vote to everyone—male or female, black or white. Becoming an excellent speaker, Belva served as president of the Universal Franchise Association.

During this time, the 37-year-old Belva met Dr. Ezekiel Lockwood, a 65-year-old dentist. Sharing similar progressive ideas, the two fell in love and were married in 1868. Together they organized a Washington chapter of the Equal Rights Association. In 1870, Belva Lockwood petitioned Congress to give female government workers equal pay for equal work. In 1872, Congress passed a bill stating that all employees of the federal government must be paid according to their positions of employment and contributions, with no differences because of their sex.

Lockwood's 1869 decision to become a lawyer would become the turning point of her life. Columbian College Law School (now George Washington University) turned her down, claiming that having women in classes would distract the men. But when Washington's National University Law School opened its classes to women in 1871, Lockwood enrolled and became one of two women to complete their studies in May 1873. However, when the male students refused to share the graduation platform with their female classmates, the school did not award the women their diplomas.

After briefly taking classes at Howard University— where Charlotte Ray, the first black woman to become a lawyer, had graduated in 1872—Lockwood decided to try again to get her diploma from National University. Since President Ulysses S. Grant served as honorary president of the law school, Lockwood wrote directly to him in the autumn of 1873. In her letter, she pointed out that she had completed all of her requirements for graduation, and, therefore, was entitled to the degree. Although President Grant never replied, she received her law school diploma a week later.

At the age of 42, Belva Lockwood was finally a lawyer. Most of her early clients were white women, but as time passed, men and minorities also came to her for legal help. Lockwood's first client was Mary Ann Folker, a mother of two children who wanted a divorce because her husband frequently became drunk and beat her.

Because Folker's husband had beaten his wife throughout their 10-year marriage, Lockwood was convinced that his wife and children needed legal protection. Lockwood filed divorce papers on September 29, 1873, charging Frederick Folker with drunkenness, cruel treatment, desertion, and refusal to support his family.

Lockwood won the case and obtained a divorce for Mary Ann Folker. The judge also granted Mrs. Folker *alimony*, or financial support, and attorney's fees, but her ex-husband refused to pay. Once again, Lockwood took the case to court. A court order directed Frederick Folker to pay the alimony, and he was sent to prison when he again refused. Within a week, he changed his mind and began to make payments.

Another early case that was well publicized in the local newspapers was Lockwood's defense of a woman who had been accused of shooting a law officer. The woman admitted her guilt when Lockwood put her on the witness stand. "Gentlemen of the jury," Lockwood began, as she rose to address the court, "the laws must be enforced. My client has committed the double offense of resisting an officer of the law and shooting a man." However, she continued, "the District [of Columbia] is under the common law. That law says a woman must obey her husband. Her husband told [my client] to load a gun and shoot the first officer that tried to force his way into the house. She obeyed him." Lockwood concluded her argument by stating that under common law, the husband, in effect, loaded the gun, and shot the officer. "You would not have a woman resist her husband?" Lockwood asked the all-male jury.

The jury returned a verdict of "not guilty." Using a law that she personally believed was wrong, Lockwood had saved a woman who was clearly guilty. Her defense demonstrated, however, that existing laws were inadequate because they didn't make women responsible for their actions.

Lockwood continued to represent impoverished clients and took on more and more pension and claims cases. Decisions in these cases were often appealed to the U.S. Court of Claims, but Lockwood was not allowed to appear before this court because it had ruled "that a woman is without legal capacity to take the office of attorney." Instead, Lockwood had to hire a male lawyer to plead her clients' cases in the Court of Claims. When Lockwood appealed this decision to the U.S. Supreme Court, the Court also turned down her petition to practice before both the Court of Claims and the Supreme Court. Lockwood recalled, "For the first time in my life I began to realize that it was a crime to be a woman; but it was too late to put in a denial, and I at once pleaded guilty to the charge of the court."

Because only special legislation by Congress could open the high courts to women attorneys, Lockwood drafted a bill that was introduced in Congress in December 1877. The bill proposed that any woman who had been "a member of the bar of the highest court of any state or territory or of the Supreme Court of the District of Columbia for the space of three years" and had "maintained a good standing before such court" and displayed "good moral character" should be allowed to practice before the U.S. Supreme Court.

Lockwood's bill was introduced in the House of Representatives by a congressman who was sympathetic to her cause. It passed easily in the House in 1878 but then died in the Senate Judiciary Committee. After being reintroduced three times, the bill finally reached the Senate floor. It passed on February 7, 1879, and was signed into law by President Rutherford B. Hayes.

Belva Lockwood, who had spent five years trying to get a law passed that would allow women to argue cases before the Supreme Court, became the first woman to practice before the Court. During those years, her husband and a new baby daughter had died, but she had not allowed her personal pain to deter her from her fight.

In 1880, Lockwood expanded her efforts and sponsored the admission of a black attorney, Samuel R. Lowery, to practice before the Supreme Court. He became the fourth black man admitted to the Court, the first from the South.

Lockwood also continued to lecture, write, and work for women's rights. Disappointed at the lack of concern shown by the major political parties for women's issues, in 1884 Lockwood asked in a public letter to a friend, women's rights leader Susan B. Anthony, "Why not nominate women for important places: Is not [Queen]

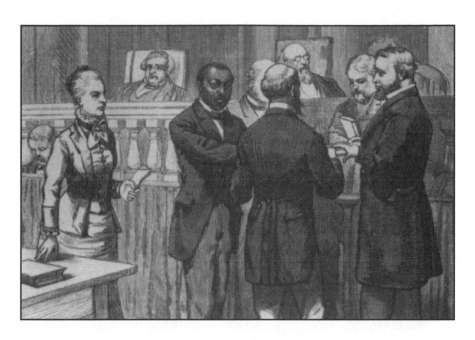

The year after Lockwood (left) finally gained entrance to the U.S. Supreme Court in 1879, she sponsored the admission of Samuel Lowery, who became the first southern black lawyer to appear before the Court.

Victoria Empress of India? Have we not among our . . . women persons of as much talent and ability?" Her letter pointed out that although American women could not vote, no law kept men from voting *for* women. The time had come for women to have their own party, their own platform, and their own nominees. "We shall never have rights until we take them, nor respect until we command it," Lockwood predicted.

As a result of her letter, which was published in newspapers across the country, the Equal Rights Party nominated Lockwood as its 1884 presidential candidate. This made her the first woman to appear on a national ballot and to campaign actively in a presidential election.

Lockwood's running mate was Marietta Stow, editor of a women's rights newspaper in California.

In accepting the nomination, Lockwood pledged "to do . . . justice to every class of our citizens, without distinction of color, sex, or nationality." She promised to fight for free education and higher wages for all, the appointment of a competent woman to the U.S. Supreme Court, pensions for disabled soldiers, and full citizenship rights for American Indians.

During her presidential campaign, Lockwood gave interviews and made speeches at campaign rallies across the country. Some newspapers supported her candidacy; others criticized it or made fun of it. The *Lockport Daily Union* published the following poem:

> My soul is tired of politics,
> Its vicious ways, its knavish tricks;
> I will not vote for any man
> But whoop it up for Belva Ann.

Although the election was won by Democrat Grover Cleveland, Lockwood received 4,149 popular votes—all cast by men since women were not allowed to vote. In 1888, the Equal Rights Party renominated Lockwood as its presidential candidate. This time, Lockwood ran with Alfred H. Love on a ticket of peace and women's rights but did not receive as many votes as in 1884.

From the mid-1880s on, Lockwood increasingly devoted her energies to the cause of universal peace. Her presidential platform had included peace initiatives; now she became an officer in the Universal Peace Union and was a five-time delegate to the International Peace Conference.

Throughout the 1880s and 1890s, Lockwood also maintained a busy law practice. In 1891, she took on one of the most significant cases of her career—the claim of 15,000 Cherokees of the eastern states against the U.S. government. Lockwood would work on the case for 14 years. She prepared by studying the historical relationship between the U.S. government and the Cherokee Nation since the early nineteenth century.

The original home of the Cherokees had been the Great Smoky Mountains, which extended from Tennessee and North Carolina into Georgia. In the decade from 1817 to 1827, the Cherokees had established the Cherokee Nation with a constitution and a democratic form of government. Like the U.S. government, the Cherokees had placed voting power in the hands of the people and divided the government into three branches to ensure a balance of power: the executive branch (a chief), the legislative branch (a house of representatives and a senate), and the judicial branch (a supreme court). The Cherokee Nation had hoped to gain respect and recognition from the U.S. government.

The Cherokees had prospered under this form of government, but as white settlers pushed further west, they eyed the Cherokees' valuable land. When gold was discovered in Cherokee territory, the settlers urged the U.S. government to obtain the land. In 1830, Congress passed the Indian Removal Bill, which provided for resettling American Indian tribes in territory that is now the state of Oklahoma. Although some Indians voluntarily relocated, most did not.

The 1835 Treaty of New Echota, from which the Cherokee claim had originated, was signed by only 79 of the thousands of Cherokees who lived in the Great Smoky Mountain Range. The U.S. government promised to pay the tribal members for their land if they would turn it over and move west within three years. Although the vast majority of Cherokees did not sign the treaty and many Americans saw it as fraudulent, the government considered the treaty a legal and binding document.

In 1832, before the Treaty of New Echota, the Cherokee Nation had brought a case against Georgia to the Supreme Court. Chief Justice John Marshall had upheld the independence of the Cherokee Nation, which meant that Georgia laws designed to push the Cherokees off their land were invalid. But President Andrew Jackson ignored Marshall's decision, and the state of Georgia used military force to expel the Cherokees. The Georgia militia rounded up 14,000 Cherokees and marched them west in the winter of 1838—a march that has been named the "Trail of Tears" because 4,000 Cherokees perished along the way.

During the years that followed, the Cherokees had never received the purchase price specified in the Treaty of New Echota. Finally, at the end of the century, Lockwood represented the descendants of the eastern Cherokees (other attorneys represented the Cherokees of Oklahoma) who were attempting to recover their original share and the interest it had earned. More than 1,000

Although the U.S. Congress passed an Indian Removal Bill in 1830, the Cherokees fought the law successfully in the courts. In 1838, however, they were forced to leave their beloved land, and thousands died from exhaustion, exposure, and disease along the "Trail of Tears."

Cherokees had escaped the soldiers in 1838 by hiding in North Carolina's Great Smoky Mountains. In 1891, their descendants signed a treaty that allowed them to work their land legally. Now Lockwood's help was sought to collect the money that was owed these families.

The 1835 Treaty of New Echota had set the purchase price of the Cherokee land at $1 million. The U.S. government did not dispute this figure. The claim brought by the Cherokees in 1891, however, also included interest, which brought the total to almost $5 million—or five times the original price.

Early in 1905, after 14 years of research and preparation, the case of the eastern and emigrant Cherokees against the United States was heard in the Court of Claims before Judge Charles Nott, the same judge who had opposed Lockwood's admission to the court more than 30 years earlier. On March 20, Nott delivered the opinion of the court. Although he acknowledged that the government had broken the Treaty of New Echota, he refused to award the full interest that was claimed.

Lockwood next appealed to the U.S. Supreme Court. Backing her arguments with the facts and figures she had accumulated during her years of research, the 75-year-old Lockwood stated that the Cherokees deserved full payment from the government because they had been forced from their homes and had suffered tremendously at the hands of the government. She next pointed out that the Cherokees had not read the treaty, had not signed it, and had not been a party in its negotiation. The Supreme Court justices who heard the case later agreed that Lockwood had made "the most eloquent argument of any of the attorneys before the Court."

On April 30, 1906, Chief Justice Melville Fuller declared that the United States should pay the 15,000 Cherokee claimants the $1 million purchase price plus nearly $4 million of accumulated interest for a total settlement of almost $5 million. Newspapers said the case was the largest claim ever made against the government.

Lockwood retired from her law practice in 1914 at the age of 84 but continued her work for world peace and women's rights. Believing that President Woodrow

Belva Lockwood was active in the women's suffrage movement until the end of her life. At age 83, she led a suffrage march into U.S. congressional chambers.

Wilson would keep the United States out of World War I, Lockwood was active in his 1916 reelection campaign—and was deeply disillusioned by Wilson's decision to enter World War I five months following his election.

Lockwood died on May 19, 1917, at the age of 86. Three years later, women finally won the right to vote. Lockwood's determination, persistence, and courage had opened up law schools and the courts to women who chose to enter them. She was an organizer, an activist, and a role model in the struggle for equality, living by her own motto, "Fight, fight, fight everlastingly."

Clarence Seward Darrow (1857–1938) seemed destined to defend the defenseless. He recalled visits to his family's "station" on the Underground Railroad from runaway slaves and from John Brown, a white man who was executed for trying to start a slave rebellion.

5

Clarence Darrow
Voice of the Outcasts

*I*n 1925, Clarence Darrow heard that William Jennings Bryan had volunteered to represent the state in the *Tennessee v. Scopes* trial. Immediately, Darrow and his friend Dudley Field Malone, a New York attorney, sent a telegram to the lawyer representing John Scopes. It read, "In case you should need us, we are willing, without fees or expense, to help the defense of Scopes in any way you may suggest or direct."

Because Darrow was so controversial, the American Civil Liberties Union (ACLU), which was representing Scopes, was concerned about using him as counsel for

81

the defense. The defendant, 24-year-old John Scopes, a biology teacher in Dayton, Tennessee, on trial for teaching evolution, made the final decision. "It's going to be a gouging, roughhouse battle," he said. "If it's going to be a gutter fight, I'd rather have a good gutter fighter."

As advanced by British scientist Charles Darwin, the theory of evolution stated that life on earth, including human life, had developed over a period of millions of years. Religious fundamentalists, however, said that evolutionists placed Darwin's theory above the words of God and ridiculed them for believing that humans had evolved from apes. The fundamentalists believed in a literal interpretation of the biblical story of Genesis—that God had created the world and everything in it in just six days.

After World War I, fundamentalist Christians in the South lobbied state legislatures to pass anti-evolution laws because they did not want children to be taught beliefs that the fundamentalists found to be contrary to the Bible. They believed that evolution contradicted the biblical story of God's creation of life and taught that humans had come from lower forms of animals. Florida was the first state to pass a law forbidding the teaching of evolution in public schools, and Tennessee adopted a similar law on March 21, 1925.

William Jennings Bryan, a three-time presidential candidate and a former secretary of state, was a leader of the fundamentalists. His goal was to pass anti-evolution bills in two-thirds of the states and then to have Congress add an amendment to the U.S. Constitution that would outlaw the teaching of evolution in all U.S. schools.

Darrow had twice supported the presidential campaigns of William Jennings Bryan (1860-1925) and shared his sympathies for laborers and farmers.

The ACLU feared that more states would follow the example of Florida and Tennessee. They and people like Clarence Darrow believed that constitutional protection for freedom of speech and the separation of church and state were threatened. In their eyes, Bryan and the fundamentalists were attempting to force their particular religious beliefs upon the rest of the country.

The ACLU was willing to challenge the constitutionality of the law by financing a test case. In Dayton,

Tennessee, businessman George Rappelyea, who opposed the anti-evolution bill, approached John Scopes, the biology teacher at the local high school. Believing that it was impossible to teach biology without talking about evolution, Scopes agreed to be the test case defendant and volunteered to be arrested for teaching evolution.

Some leaders of the ACLU thought a conservative attorney with a traditional religious background should defend Scopes. They were concerned that having Darrow as a defense attorney would make the trial a battle over religion instead of a defense of the freedom of speech and the separation of church and state. Darrow was the most famous and possibly the greatest criminal lawyer in America at that time, and he was also an outspoken *agnostic*—a person who believes that it is impossible to prove the existence of God. Darrow believed that organized religion limited human knowledge and freedom by telling people what they should think and believe.

Clarence Seward Darrow was born in Farmdale, Ohio, on April 18, 1857, and grew up in nearby Kinsman. His father had graduated from a Unitarian seminary in Pennsylvania but soon left the church, resigning from the ministry to become a furniture maker and the town's undertaker. Because the former minister loved reading and ideas more than business, it was his wife who kept the furniture shop running. She also was active in the women's suffrage movement. Both were idealists whose sympathies lay with the poor and the oppressed.

Darrow was especially close to his father. He once wrote: "More than anything else, my father influenced the course of my life and its thought and activities." Because the Darrows did not attend church regularly, they were looked upon as different by some of their neighbors. This experience and his reading taught Clarence to be an independent thinker and not to be concerned about the opinions of others.

Darrow left Ohio to attend Allegheny College in Meadville, Pennsylvania. After studying there for a year, he taught school for three years while reading law. Darrow then spent a year at the University of Michigan Law School and completed his legal training at a law office in Youngstown, Ohio.

In 1878, Darrow began to practice law in Ohio, first in Andover, and then in Ashtabula, where he moved with his new wife, Jessie. There he was elected city *solicitor*, or chief law officer, and began to shape his political and social philosophies. He was influenced by Henry George, who in *Progress and Poverty* supported a single tax on land earnings, believing that such a tax would lead to social equality and opportunity. Another book, John Peter Altgeld's *Our Penal Machinery and Its Victims*, influenced Darrow's ideas about crime. Because most criminals were poor, he became convinced that crime resulted from poverty and the lack of opportunity.

Darrow and his wife moved to Chicago in 1888, where he was appointed corporation counsel for the city. Several years later, he became corporation counsel for the Chicago and Northwestern Railway Company.

In 1894, the American Railway Union, whose president was Eugene V. Debs, supported the railway workers

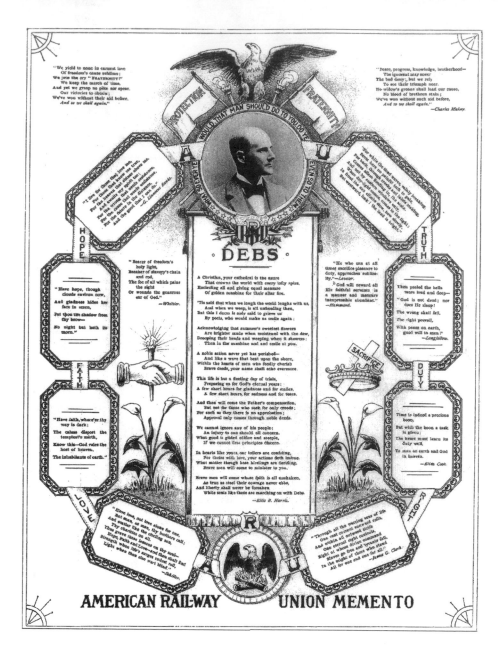

Although the American Railway Union's action in support of the Pullman workers was dubbed "Debs' Rebellion," Eugene V. Debs (1855-1926) had actually argued against the strike.

in their strike against the Pullman Sleeping Car Company. Federal prosecutors indicted Debs and several other board members for conspiracy against the Pullman Sleeping Car Company and for violation of an anti-strike injunction—a court order prohibiting harassment, violence, or any interference with the U.S. mail (which was delivered by train) during a strike. Darrow sympathized with Debs and resigned his position with the railway company to become his attorney.

That move was a turning point in Darrow's life. With the defense of Debs, he became involved in the labor movement—a relationship that would last for many years. Darrow denounced the railroad company for using the word "conspiracy," a word that was a "favorite weapon of every tyrant." Darrow told the court that every free man had the right to decide for himself whether to leave his job for any reason.

The conspiracy case against Debs was dismissed after a juror fell ill, but he did spend six months in jail for civil contempt because he had ignored a court order to stop all strike-related activities. Darrow's defense of Debs had established him as the nation's leading labor attorney.

Darrow's next notable labor case was in 1898 when he defended Thomas Kidd, the general secretary of the Amalgamated Woodworkers International Union. In Oshkosh, Wisconsin, Kidd had organized a 14-week strike against the Paine Lumber Company, the country's largest manufacturer of window sashes, doors, and blinds. Woodworkers at Paine walked off their jobs, demanding better wages and a weekly paycheck as well as recognition for their union and the prohibition of child and women's labor. Owner George Paine refused to meet with union representatives and accused Kidd of criminal conspiracy against the company.

Darrow told the jury in the Kidd trial that the so-called conspiracy was instead a labor union. He insisted, "every intelligent person understands that workingmen have the right to organize; understands that if laborers are not satisfied with their condition, they may stop work; they may stop work singly or collectively." After a dramatic and emotionally powerful two-day summation, Darrow concluded by saying the verdict would "be a milestone in the history of the world, and an inspiration and hope to the dumb, despairing millions whose faith is in your hands." The jury deliberated for 50 minutes and returned a "not guilty" verdict for Kidd.

The labor movement once again turned to Darrow in 1902 after the United Mine Workers went on strike in the Pennsylvania coal mines. As chief counsel for the coal miners in compulsory and binding arbitration before a board appointed by President Theodore Roosevelt, Darrow helped to gain for his clients a ruling for a 10 percent pay increase, a 9-hour work day (reduced from 12 hours), and overtime pay.

In 1911, Darrow defended two brothers, John J. and James B. McNamara, who were implicated in a series of bombings by a fellow conspirator. The most serious charge against the two was an explosion at the *Los Angeles Times* building, which had killed 20 and left dozens injured. Because both brothers were union activists,

Harrison Gray Otis, the owner of the newspaper, blamed the unions for the bombing and the fire it had ignited.

Darrow accepted the case with reluctance because he was in poor health from a near-fatal ear infection. After months of investigation, Darrow believed that his union clients were guilty and had almost no chance of winning. Therefore, he worked out a plea bargain. In exchange for avoiding the death penalty, James would plead guilty to the *Times* blast, and John would plead guilty to the bombing of the Llewellyn Iron Works, in which no one was injured. James was sentenced to life in prison, and John received a 15-year prison sentence. Although the leaders of the labor movement initially felt betrayed by the change of plea, they denounced the bombings and eventually regained their trust in Darrow, even honoring him the following year on Labor Day.

Two months after the trial, Darrow was accused of bribing some of the jurors in the McNamara case. Facing indictments on two separate bribery charges, Darrow believed his best defense was his lack of motive. Why bribe jurors when his clients had already pleaded guilty? Darrow insisted he was on trial only because he was a "lover of the poor, a friend of the oppressed" and because he had represented labor concerns for so many years.

The jury in the first bribery trial deliberated for only 30 minutes. When they returned, the foreman announced that Darrow had been found "not guilty." In the second trial, the jury was deadlocked, and the judge dismissed the case. Darrow's guilt or innocence of the jury bribery charges is still being debated today.

In 1920, Darrow defended 20 Communists from Chicago who had been indicted on the grounds that Communism advocated the violent overthrow of the U.S. government. Darrow insisted on the rights of the Communist Party to exist and of the the defendants to express their views. Although the jury convicted the 20 men, the governor of Illinois pardoned them two years later while their conviction was still being appealed.

In one of the most sensational cases of his career, Darrow defended the sons of two Chicago millionaires who tried to commit the "perfect" murder. The defendants were 18-year-old Nathan Leopold Jr., a University of Chicago graduate and the son of a wealthy box manufacturer, and 17-year-old Richard Loeb, a University of Michigan honors graduate and the son of a vice-president of Sears, Roebuck & Company. They had already confessed to the kidnapping and murder of 14-year-old Bobby Franks, a distant relative of Loeb and the son of a wealthy Chicago industrialist. The boys' parents begged Darrow to defend their sons to save them from hanging.

One of the reasons the 67-year-old attorney took the case was that it provided him with a public platform to argue against capital punishment. Taking Darrow's advice, Leopold and Loeb pleaded guilty to the charges of kidnapping and murder. Thus, there would be no jury. Only a judge would hear the case and determine the sentence. Darrow planned to argue for leniency.

During the trial, Darrow introduced psychiatric evidence—the first time that such evidence formed the major part of the defense in a murder trial. Defense psychiatrists stated that both Leopold and Loeb were emotionally stunted and unable to distinguish right from wrong. Loeb was a thrill-seeker, willing to commit murder for the sake of a new experience. Leopold believed in the theories of German philosopher Friedrich Nietzsche and considered himself a "superman"—someone superior to others and thus above the law.

Many criticized Darrow for taking the Leopold-Loeb case, calling him a hypocrite and a sell out. But Darrow believed that the two boys were mentally ill and products of their heredity and environment. The families of these wealthy boys had never given them any concept

Although the public feared that Nathan Leopold (left) and Richard Loeb would not be convicted of murder, Darrow pledged, "In no event will the families use money in an attempt to defeat justice."

of responsibility or social obligations. As a result, they believed that they could do exactly as they pleased.

In his closing argument, Darrow stated, "The easy thing and the popular thing" would be to hang the two young men. But he asked the judge to take into account their youth and pleaded for "life, understanding, charity, kindness, and the infinite mercy that considers all."

Judge John Caverly announced his decision on September 10, 1924. He sentenced the two boys to life in prison instead of hanging, explaining he had been moved to make this decision "chiefly by the consideration of the age of the defendants." To the two young men, "the prolonged suffering of years of confinement . . . [might seem] the severer form of retribution."

Darrow's next case, the Scopes trial in Tennessee, was nothing short of a public spectacle. In the summer of 1925, the town of Dayton assumed a circus-like atmosphere, and the trial was quickly dubbed the "Monkey Trial." Religious fundamentalists and newspaper reporters roamed the streets, and newly built lemonade and hot-dog stands crowded the sidewalks. Trained monkeys were even paraded up and down the streets.

In a speech before the trial, William Jennings Bryan, who had not tried a case in nearly 40 years, stated, "If evolution wins in Dayton, Christianity goes."

"Scopes isn't on trial," Darrow responded to Bryan's comments. "Civilization is on trial. . . . No man's belief will be safe."

The trial began on July 10, 1925, in the Eighteenth Tennessee Circuit Court with Judge John T. Raulston presiding. The jury was quickly selected and then excused while the lawyers argued about the indictment and questions of constitutionality. With his typical eloquence, Darrow declared, "If today you can take a thing like evolution and make it a crime to teach it in the public school," tomorrow it could be a crime to teach evolution anywhere else. He warned that if the trend of banning unpopular ideas continued, then certain groups might next try to "ban books and newspapers" and "foist [their] own religion upon others." The result, Darrow predicted, would be nonstop fighting among people and religious groups. If teaching evolution were wrong, he concluded, the country might as well go back to the sixteenth century, when people "who dared to bring any intelligence and enlightenment and culture to the human mind" were burned by bigots. The spectators hissed at Darrow, and, as expected, the judge refused to throw out the indictment against Scopes.

Then the jury was brought in, and the trial began. Despite Darrow's opposition, Raulston opened each session with a prayer, and both the judge and Bryan gave what amounted to sermons at various times throughout the trial. Darrow wanted to show that evolution did not necessarily conflict with the biblical story of creation, and he planned to put prominent scientists and religion experts on the stand to explain the theory of evolution and its relationship to the Bible. Judge Raulston, however, ruled that their testimony would not be admitted. Instead, this evidence was submitted as written statements that were read into the record.

In the hot courtroom during the Scopes trial, tempers often flared. When Darrow became angry because Judge Raulston wouldn't allow scientists and religion experts to appear in court, he was cited for contempt.

On Monday, July 20, the seventh day of the trial, Darrow took everyone by surprise by calling William Jennings Bryan to the stand as an expert witness on the Bible. Calling an opposing attorney as a witness was extremely unusual, but Bryan agreed to testify. The stage was now set for a dramatic clash between the two men.

The confrontation began quietly. But as Darrow fired question after question at Bryan, who declared that he believed every word in the Bible in a literal sense, the 65-year-old former presidential candidate became confused and uncertain. Contradicting what he had previously stated, he eventually conceded that some parts of the creation story could be interpreted in different ways. For example, he acknowledged that the six days of creation could have been millions of years instead of 24-hour days.

At times, the questioning became so heated that both men were screaming and shaking their fists at each other. The crowd laughed as Darrow mocked Bryan. After two hours, Bryan left the witness stand, a broken and bewildered man. Instead of being pleased, Darrow was saddened by the demise of this once influential statesman whom he had admired. Five days after the trial was over, William Jennings Bryan would die in his sleep.

The day after Bryan testified, Judge Raulston ordered his testimony stricken from the record. Darrow then requested that the judge "instruct the jury to find the defendant guilty." Darrow wanted his client to be declared "guilty" because he planned to appeal the "guilty" verdict to a higher court to test the constitutionality of the anti-evolution law.

The jury found Scopes "guilty," and the judge fined him $100. The young teacher then spoke for the first time in the trial. "Your honor," he said, "I feel that I have been convicted of violating an unjust statute. I will continue in the future, as I have in the past, to oppose this law in any way I can. Any other action would be in violation of my ideal of academic freedom—that is, to teach the truth as guaranteed in our constitution, of personal and religious freedom."

In 1927, the Tennessee Supreme Court declared the 1925 Butler Act—the law that had made it unlawful to

Soon after the trial, John T. Scopes stopped teaching and went to graduate school—with a scholarship set up by the expert witnesses for the defense, who had appreciated his role in the test case.

teach evolution in Tennessee schools—to be constitutional. However, they overturned Scopes's conviction on a technicality, stating that the jury, not the judge, should have set the fine. Since the conviction was overturned, the ACLU could not take the case to a higher court. Although the anti-evolution law remained in force for 42 years, there was never any attempt to try Scopes again or anyone else who taught evolution. In 1967, the Tennessee legislature finally repealed the Butler Act.

In 1926, Darrow participated in what he considered to be his most important case. Dr. Ossian Sweet and ten other blacks were accused of murdering a white man who was part of a mob outside Dr. Sweet's house. The victim had been a member of the Water Works Improvement Association, a neighborhood group organized by the Ku Klux Klan that had been trying to force the Sweets out of their home.

On the night of the killing, a large crowd of whites had surrounded the Sweet home, throwing stones, breaking windows, and threatening the lives of the people inside. Speaking on behalf of his clients, Darrow argued that the Sweets and their friends had acted in self-defense against the mob. Darrow told the jury that he spoke "for a million blacks who have some hope and faith remaining in the institutions of this land." He asked the jurors "to do justice in this case." The jury was deadlocked and could not reach a verdict. The jury in the second trial, however, took only a few hours to decide that the 11 black defendants were "not guilty."

During the last years of his life, Darrow took an occasional case, engaged in public speaking and debates, read, wrote, and traveled. America's greatest criminal lawyer died on March 13, 1938, at the age of 80.

According to lawyer Daniel Kornstein, Darrow "turned his clients into universal symbols," using them to shed light on "recurring themes" in U.S. history: "social justice, redistribution of wealth, the labor movement, tolerance and freedom of thought, the role of religion in public schools, the death penalty, race relations."

Robert H. Jackson (1892-1954) was the last U.S. Supreme Court justice to obtain his legal training through "reading law" with a lawyer instead of graduating from a law school.

6

Robert H. Jackson
International Prosecutor

*T*wo weeks after the death of Franklin D. Roosevelt on April 12, 1945, President Harry S. Truman set in motion one of the most important trials in world history when he asked U.S. Supreme Court Justice Robert H. Jackson to be the chief U.S. prosecutor in the Nazi war-crimes trials.

Throughout World War II, Germany had defied the rules of the Hague and Geneva Conventions, which defined and outlawed war crimes. The Germans had also ignored the Allied powers when they were warned in 1942 and again in 1943 that those responsible for war crimes, notably the murder of millions of Jews, would be punished. Furthermore, German dictator Adolf Hitler had not listened to President Roosevelt when he declared on March 24, 1944, that "none who participate in these acts of savagery shall go unpunished." Hitler and the Nazis had been convinced they would win the war. As victors, they would not have to answer to anyone. But now the war was almost over and Germany was nearly defeated.

Despite the fact that legal precedents were scant and the body of law had scarcely been tested, Justice Jackson decided to take on the difficult job of conducting the war-crimes trials. For the first time, U.S. laws involving conspiracy and guilt by association (such as those used to incriminate the labor leaders whom Clarence Darrow had defended) would be used in international courts. Also untried were the application of the Kellogg-Briand Pact,

The most despised war criminal, German dictator Adolf Hitler, committed suicide on April 30, 1945, four days after Jackson was appointed U.S. prosecutor for the war-crimes trials.

which outlawed "aggressive" war (starting a war without provocation), and indictments for prewar crimes against humanity. Jackson later said he had accepted the job because "to represent the government in an international trial, the first of its kind in history, was a challenge that no man who loved advocacy could pass up willingly."

On February 13, 1892, Robert Houghwout Jackson was born in Spring Creek, Pennsylvania, where his family raised horses. When Robert was five, the family moved to the Jamestown area of western New York.

As a teenager, Jackson loved to read. After he graduated from high school in 1910, Jackson made the unusual decision to attend another nearby high school for a year to study literature and debate. At the same time, he began reading law in the offices of Frank Mott, a local attorney and distant cousin. There Jackson did legal research and helped in the drafting of *briefs*, or lists of facts and points of law relevant to pending cases. He also attended the Albany Law School for one year, earning a certificate because he was not yet old enough to be awarded a law degree. Most of his afternoons were spent listening to arguments in the New York Court of Appeals.

In 1913, at age 21, Jackson passed the bar exam and opened his own practice in Jamestown. He later described himself as a country lawyer who learned from other lawyers. "In those days," he recalled, "the lawyers gathered and discussed cases and pointed out where somebody made a mistake." Jackson later said that he "absorbed a great deal by association with these experienced older men."

Jackson practiced law in Jamestown for more than 20 years. He was a lawyer for the city and also represented the local bank, railway and telephone companies, and other industries. He also took on many criminal cases. Although Jackson had several partnership offers from large and prestigious New York City law firms, he and his family preferred to remain in Jamestown.

In Jamestown, Jackson was a lone Democrat in a Republican area. As a member of the Democratic State Committee, he was active in party politics and became acquainted with Franklin Roosevelt when the future president served as assistant secretary of the navy (1913-1920). When he was elected governor of New York in 1920, Roosevelt offered Jackson an appointment to the Public Service Commission, but Jackson declined. Roosevelt became president in 1933 and the following year asked Jackson to become general counsel to the Bureau of Internal Revenue (now the Internal Revenue Service). This time, Jackson accepted.

Jackson rose quickly in the Roosevelt administration and, in 1935, he was appointed special counsel for the Securities and Exchange Commission. The following year, he became head of the tax division of the Justice Department and then assistant attorney general in charge of the antitrust division. He was appointed U.S. *solicitor general*, or government representative before the Supreme Court, in 1938 and won almost every case he argued before the Supreme Court. Many of these cases helped to defend the constitutionality of President Roosevelt's New Deal legislation.

During this time, Jackson wrote *The Struggle for Judicial Supremacy*, which outlined the legal difficulties that the Roosevelt administration faced because of decisions made by the Supreme Court. In a later interview, Jackson stated that the Court's justices were "applying the standards of their youth to the legislation of an entirely different period" and thus "were striking down a good deal of legislation on the basis of what conditions were when they were brought up on the frontier."

Jackson enjoyed his term as solicitor general, calling it "the highest prize that would come to a lawyer." He felt the office offered him an opportunity to shape "the position that the government . . . [would] take on many legal issues."

Jackson's most notable case as solicitor general was his successful defense of the Social Security Act of 1935, which provided for old-age pensions and unemployment compensation. Believing that the problem of poverty among the elderly was too widespread for the states to handle and that the 1935 law did not take power away from the states, but "provide[d] for the general welfare," Jackson argued for a strong federal government to help solve the nationwide economic problems created by the Great Depression of the 1930s.

In January 1940, Jackson was appointed to Roosevelt's cabinet as attorney general, and he also began serving as one of the president's personal advisors. In his new capacity, Jackson gave Roosevelt advice about the legality of the lend-lease program that would send U.S. destroyers from World War I to the British for use in their war with Germany. In exchange for the destroyers, Great Britain would allow the United States to use British air and naval bases throughout the world.

Robert Jackson was named an associate justice of the U.S. Supreme Court in 1941. His responsibilities as a Supreme Court justice were dramatically different from the advocacy role of the solicitor general. In later years, Jackson would complain that on the Monday following the December 7, 1941, attack on Pearl Harbor, the Court heard arguments about whether country club members could be taxed on their greens fees at golf courses.

One of Jackson's best-known opinions from his 13 years as a Supreme Court justice was *West Virginia State Board of Education v. Barnette* (1943). This civil liberties case was an example of Jackson's defense of the individual against the state. In the 1940 case of *Minersville School District v. Gobitis*, the Supreme Court had ruled against a family of Jehovah's Witnesses who objected to saluting the flag in school because their religion claimed that doing so was bowing down to an idol—an act forbidden by one of the Ten Commandments. In *Barnette*, the Court overturned this earlier decision, ruling that forcing school children who were Jehovah's Witnesses to salute the flag was unconstitutional. Jackson wrote the majority opinion in *Barnette*. He argued that "the action of the local authorities in compelling the flag salute and pledge transcends constitutional limitations on their power and invades the sphere of intellect and spirit which it is the purpose of the First Amendment to our Constitution to reserve from all official control."

104

The U.S. Supreme Court had dismissed three earlier cases and ruled against a 1940 case challenging school requirements that all students salute the U.S. flag.

In *Korematsu v. United States* (1944), the Court upheld the legality of the evacuation and internment of Americans of Japanese descent living on the West Coast, which President Roosevelt had approved as commander-in-chief. After May 9, 1942, when a military order had banned all persons of Japanese ancestry from that area, Fred Korematsu, a Japanese-American citizen, was convicted in a federal district court for remaining in San Leandro, California.

A majority of the justices on the Court ruled that excluding people from military areas was within the combined war powers of the president and Congress. Jackson, however, disagreed with the decision. He wrote the dissenting opinion in the case, noting that:

> Korematsu was born on our soil, of parents born in Japan. The Constitution makes him a citizen of the United States by nativity and a citizen of California by residence. No claim is made that he is not loyal to this country. There is no suggestion that apart from the matter involved here he is not law-abiding and well-disposed. Korematsu, however, has been convicted of an act not commonly a crime. It consists merely of being present in the state whereof he is a citizen, near the place where he was born, and where all his life he has lived.

After the December 7, 1941, bombing of Pearl Harbor, Japanese-Americans living on the West Coast were forced to leave their homes, businesses, and employment and remain in internment camps for the duration of the war.

Even though he had been appointed to the Supreme Court by President Roosevelt, whom he admired, Jackson maintained his conviction that the internment was unjust. The Court, he contended, had construed Korematsu's action as a crime only because he had Japanese parents.

Jackson's next assignment was the war-crimes trials, which he regarded as the most significant work of his career. He took a leave of absence from the U.S. Supreme Court and traveled to London to become chief U.S. prosecutor at the trials.

In the London Agreement of August 1945, the United States, Great Britain, France, and the Soviet Union pledged to prosecute and punish the major war criminals of World War II. An international military tribunal was established with four judges, one from each of the participating countries, and four alternates. This tribunal would consider three specific types of acts as war crimes: 1) the waging of an aggressive war; 2) violations of the laws of war such as ill-treatment of civilians, murder of hostages and prisoners of war, and the unnecessary destruction of property; and 3) the murder, extermination, or enslavement of the civilian population. The application of conspiracy laws meant the Nazi leaders who had ordered these actions would be held accountable for them.

The defendants included 22 top Nazis, whose titles and actual power had shifted according to Hitler's whims. Among them were Hermann Göring, commander of the air force and second in command to Adolf Hitler; Rudolf Hess, deputy to Hitler; Joachim von Ribbentrop, foreign minister; Alfred Jodl, chief of operations of the armed forces; and Wilhelm Keitel, chief of staff of the armed forces. Each man had his own attorney and could take the stand in his own defense. Also on trial were leaders of Nazi police organizations such as the *Schutzstaffel* (SS) and the Gestapo.

Jackson selected Nuremberg, Germany, as the site for the trials. He was in charge of all the courtroom preparations, including making accommodations for the witnesses, the defendants, and the press, and arranging a system of simultaneous translation of testimony into four languages—German, English, French, and Russian. He also supervised the collection of evidence and assigned specific tasks to the four prosecution teams.

The potential evidence against the Nazis was overwhelming. The U.S. prosecution team went over more than 100,000 German documents and translated about 4,000 into four languages for use, in whole or in part, as exhibits in the trial. They examined millions of feet of motion picture film and brought over 100,000 feet to the courtroom. They also selected more than 1,800 photographs to present as evidence.

Jackson conducted the presentation of the cases before the tribunal. He decided that the documents, not just the testimony of witnesses, should be the primary basis for the cases against the war criminals. Some of his staff members believed that eyewitness accounts would be more powerful, but Jackson was convinced that captured documents, most of them written by the Nazis themselves, would provide the strongest evidence in the cases. Because the testimony of witnesses could be influenced by faulty recollection and personal bias, Jackson believed that the authenticity of the documents would settle any doubts as to what really took place. He wanted future generations to know exactly what crimes the Nazis had committed.

The entire world watched as the trials began on November 20, 1945. In his opening statement the following day, Jackson spent more than four hours outlining the Nazi conspiracy to first take over Germany and then launch an aggressive war in Europe, wiping out entire countries and putting whole groups of people to death. William Shirer, author of *The Rise and Fall of the Third Reich*, called the speech "one of the great trial addresses of history." In his statement, Jackson declared:

> The privilege of opening the first trial in history for crimes against the peace of the world imposes a grave responsibility. The wrongs which we seek to condemn and punish have been so calculated, so malignant, and so devastating, that civilization cannot tolerate their being ignored, because it cannot survive their being repeated.

Jackson warned that future generations would judge the tribunal and its decisions, and he advised his listeners to "summon such detachment and intellectual integrity to our task that this trial will commend itself to posterity as fulfilling humanity's aspirations to do justice."

The trials lasted for 10 months. Thousands of documents were read into the record, and scores of witnesses testified. The evidence detailed mass deportations and

*During the Nuremberg trials, photographs such as
this one provided concrete evidence that the Nazis had
deliberately planned and carried out the murders of
6 million Jews, as well as Gypsies, disabled people,
political dissidents, and homosexuals.*

executions of Jews, torturous medical experiments on Jewish prisoners, the use of Jews and other prisoners as slave labor in prison factories, and the killing of hostages and Russian prisoners of war. Millions had died in the various Nazi concentration camps.

The horror of the words from witnesses and German documents was surpassed only by the motion pictures—taken by the Allies and by the Germans themselves—that vividly recorded the awful brutality and mass murder. One German film showed 200 prisoners herded into a barn that was then set on fire by SS men. The few prisoners who escaped were machine-gunned to death. The tribunal viewed images of thousands of men and women who had been starved until they could barely move, bodies that had been cremated in huge ovens (including infants who were often thrown into the crematoriums alive instead of being gassed), endless stacks of skeletal remains, and corpses being shoved into mass graves by bulldozers.

In *Nuremberg: Infamy on Trial*, author Joseph Persico described the viewing of the films at the trials: "The films went on for over two hours, a phantasmagoria of broken, charred, gray bodies, ribs protruding, legs like sticks, hollow eyes gaping. When it was over, the lights went on. Silence hung like a pall over the room."

In the course of the trials, Jackson cross-examined several key witnesses, including chief defendant Hermann Göring. Some critics felt Jackson's questioning was not effective because he failed to limit Göring to specific answers about his infamous crimes.

*After stealing a plane and flying to Scotland in 1941
(apparently in an attempt to negotiate peace with
Great Britain), Hitler's deputy, Rudolf Hess, spent
most of World War II in a British prison.*

Jackson's closing argument, however, was as impressive as his opening statement. "These defendants now ask this Tribunal to say that they are not guilty of planning, executing or conspiring to commit this long list of crimes and wrongs," Jackson stated incredulously. "If you were to say of these men that they are not guilty," he continued, "it would be as true to say that there has been no war, there are no slain, there has been no crime."

The evidence was too overwhelming, and the suffering of the Nazis' victims had been too great. Of the 22 defendants, the tribunal found 19 guilty of one or more of the counts, and they acquitted 3. Twelve, including Göring, von Ribbentrop, Jodl, and Keitel, were sentenced to death by hanging. Three were sentenced to life imprisonment, and 4 were given terms of 10 to 20 years.

Sentenced to death in the Nuremberg trials, Hermann Göring (standing) committed suicide by taking cyanide pills two hours before his scheduled hanging.

Some people criticized the Nuremberg trials because the tribunal punished the defendants for acts that were not considered crimes in their country when they had occurred. That kind of punishment involved an *ex post facto* law that was specifically prohibited by the U.S. Constitution. Yet most people agreed that it was necessary to punish acts which were so inhumane and on such a huge scale. Nuremberg established an important legal precedent: Those who start an aggressive war, who kill or torture prisoners of war and civilians, and who order and carry out mass exterminations of groups of people will eventually have to answer for their crimes in a court of international law.

Jackson believed his work at Nuremberg was far more important than his years on the Supreme Court. When he returned to the Court after an absence of one and one-half years, his experiences in Germany influenced his opinions in several cases involving free speech. When he felt certain kinds of speech were too inflammatory to be tolerated, he dissented from his colleagues, arguing that "to blanket hateful and hate-stirring attacks on races and faiths under the protection of freedom of speech . . . belittles great principles of liberty."

In *Terminiello v. Chicago* (1949), which involved a hateful anti-Semitic speech, Jackson dissented from the majority opinion that upheld the right to freedom of expression, even if it were hateful and inflammatory. He questioned the protection the law should provide for such conduct, stating that the Court had "gone far toward accepting the doctrine that civil liberty means the removal of all restraints . . . and that all local attempts to maintain order are impairments of the liberty of the citizen." If the Court did not "temper its doctrinaire logic with a little practical wisdom," he felt it would soon "convert the constitutional Bill of Rights into a suicide pact."

Jackson also strongly supported an individual's right to a full and fair hearing. *Knauff v. Shaughnessy* (1950) challenged the U.S. attorney general's refusal to allow a German-born war bride of an American veteran to enter the country. Under wartime security regulations, the government denied her a hearing. The majority opinion found that the attorney general's decision was not reviewable by the courts and that the authority to exclude aliens was inherent in the executive power to manage foreign affairs. In his dissenting opinion, Jackson declared, "Now this American citizen is told he cannot bring his wife to the United States, but he will not be told why."

Jackson argued that Congress's refusal to give the woman a hearing was unjust because "it provided a cloak for the malevolent, the misinformed, the meddlesome, and the corrupt to play the role of informer undetected and uncorrected." Anyone could cast suspicion on an alien, and the alien would have little legal recourse.

Robert Jackson remained on the Supreme Court until his death from a heart attack on October 9, 1954, at age 62. To him, the Nuremberg trials were "the most important, enduring, and constructive work" of his life. They had shown that nations could cooperate in the name of justice, and they also had established important precedents outlawing military aggression and inhumane acts.

During the Army-McCarthy hearings, the American public delighted in the quick and cutting wit of Joseph Welch (1890-1960).

7

Joseph Welch
Legal Folk Hero

*I*t was 10:30 A.M. on April 22, 1954. In the caucus room of the Senate Office Building in Washington, D.C., the Army-McCarthy hearings were underway. For the next 36 days, Americans would be glued to their television sets, watching a great drama unfold. For the first time in U.S. history, the medium of television would have an impact on the political and legal process. Instead of just reading newspaper reports, 20 million viewers could judge the participants in the hearings themselves.

During the hearings, Wisconsin senator Joseph McCarthy, a powerful political figure, showed his true character to the American people. The television viewers watched the daily battle between McCarthy and the U.S. Army. During the course of the hearings, the attorney for the army, Joseph Nye Welch, an unknown 63-year-old trial lawyer from Boston, Massachusetts, would become a household name.

The U.S. Army had charged Senator McCarthy and his aides, Roy Cohn and Frank Carr, with improperly seeking preferential treatment for Private G. David Schine, a former consultant to McCarthy. McCarthy and his aides countercharged that the army was bringing charges only to force them to stop investigating communist infiltration at several military bases.

The hearings were held before the investigations subcommittee of the Senate Committee of Government Operations. McCarthy normally headed this committee, but because the senator was one of the accused, South Dakota senator Karl Mundt assumed the chairmanship for these hearings.

Joseph Welch was special counsel to the secretary of the army, Robert Stevens. Because he knew the hearings would be well publicized, Welch almost turned down the case. Nevertheless, he finally agreed to serve as the army's special counsel.

The public loved Welch, and the press focused on his personality as much as his skills. *Life* called him "a gentleman and a scholar, a man of delicate courtesy and subtle wit." According to *Newsweek*, Welch had "a wit as sly and penetrating as a dagger," and when he asked a question, he made it "sharp enough to cut a throat."

Joseph Welch was born on October 22, 1890, in Primghar, Iowa, where his parents had settled in the 1870s. As a youngster, he loved to go to the town courthouse to watch the trials. Joseph's mother, who had little formal schooling herself, was determined that at least one of her children would become educated. Young Joe was naturally bright and earned straight A's in high school because, he recalled, his "mother wouldn't settle for less."

After graduating from high school, Joe worked for two years in a real estate office and saved enough money to attend Grinnell College. He graduated from Grinnell with honors in 1914 and received a scholarship to attend Harvard Law School.

Before Welch left for Harvard, his father said to him, "It'll take a heap of money, won't it?" and then gave his son 14 years of savings—exactly $19. During his summers off from law school, Welch earned extra money by selling state maps door-to-door. He called the work "hateful" and "hard," but later admitted that it had taught him a great deal about people. He also worked as a cement-mixer operator and a waiter.

In 1917, Welch graduated among the top students at Harvard and married Judith Lyndon, who had attended Boston's Emerson College. He enlisted in the army and was still in officers' training when World War I ended, so he did not serve overseas. When the war was over, Welch was admitted to the Massachusetts bar in 1918, and he and his wife settled in the Boston area, where he worked for a year on the legal staff of the U.S. Shipping Board. In 1923, he joined the law firm of Hale and Dorr.

Over the years, Welch built a reputation as one of the shrewdest and most disciplined lawyers in Boston. Standing up at his high, old-fashioned desk, he worked on antitrust, libel, wills, estate, and tax cases. Welch admitted to owning 150 bow ties, and he wore a different one every day during the Army-McCarthy hearings.

Upon hearing that the army had asked him to represent them, Welch exclaimed, "They must be nuts!" But when the hearings began on April 22, he was carefully prepared and ready to face Senator McCarthy. The gentlemanly, polite, and witty lawyer was pitted against the intimidating, boisterous, and overbearing senator.

To understand the significance of the Army-McCarthy hearings, it is necessary to become familiar with the career of Joseph McCarthy. In the United States, the late 1940s and early 1950s was a time of suspicion and anxiety over the threat of nuclear war. Only a few years before the enemy had been the Nazis, but now the Soviet Union—an ally during World War II—was the enemy in what was called the "Cold War." The United States had become alarmed by Soviet communist expansion in nations around the world. And while in 1945 only the United States had the atomic bomb, the rapid development of nuclear weapons in the Soviet Union had led to fears that spies were passing atomic secrets.

In 1947, the House Un-American Activities Committee had opened hearings on the communist influence in the motion picture industry. Many of the accused took the Fifth Amendment, refusing to answer questions about their supposed ties to Communists. As a result, a number of them had been blacklisted and were unable to find work in Hollywood for many years.

A year later, Elizabeth Bentley, a Communist spy, named three present and former senior officials in the government as Soviet spies. Then another witness, magazine editor Whittaker Chambers, admitted that he had worked for the Communist Party in the 1930s. Chambers named Alger Hiss, a former member of the State Department and an advisor to President Franklin Roosevelt, as a fellow party member in the 1930s. At

Elizabeth Bentley (left) and Alger Hiss (far right) testified before the House Un-American Activities Committee on August 5, 1948. (In 1950, Hiss was convicted of perjury but couldn't be tried for espionage because the statute of limitations had expired.)

After his election to the U.S. Senate in 1946, Joseph McCarthy (1908-1957) wrote no major legislation and was accused of taking contributions in return for political favors.

that time, Hiss had been in government service. Suddenly, the communist threat seemed very real.

After Republican Joseph McCarthy was elected to the Senate in 1946 at the age of 37, he sought an issue that would capture the newspaper headlines and distinguish him from other politicians. He eventually found that issue in communism—a fear he had exploited in his Senate campaign to discredit his opponents, Robert La Follette Jr. and Howard McMurray. At a speech in

Wheeling, West Virginia, on February 9, 1950, McCarthy waved a sheet of paper and declared:

> While I cannot take time to name all the men in the State Department who have been named as active members of the Communist Party and members of a spy ring, I have here in my hand a list of 205—a list of names that were made known to the Secretary of State as being members of the Communist Party and who nevertheless are still working and shaping policy in the State Department.

McCarthy's claim made him an instant celebrity. Over the succeeding weeks, he changed the figure of 205 Party members to 57 and then to 81. He made speech after speech about Communists in high levels of government but offered no proof to back up his claims. When one charge fell apart, he would produce yet another more sensational claim. (Today the term "McCarthyism" has come to mean attacks on an individual or an organization that are characterized by tactics of sensationalism and unproven accusations.)

Polls showed that most Americans supported McCarthy's quest to rid the government of subversives and spies. Even the election of a fellow Republican, Dwight D. Eisenhower, to the presidency in 1952 did not stop him from casting doubt on the loyalty of government officials. He had become such a powerful man that those who publicly opposed him risked their careers.

In 1953, McCarthy appointed Roy Cohn as chief counsel to his investigations subcommittee. Soon, on

Cohn's recommendation, McCarthy hired G. David Schine as an unpaid chief consultant. When the army drafted Schine, Cohn tried to get his friend a commission as an officer with special privileges.

McCarthy, meanwhile, initiated an attack on the army to prove that Fort Monmouth, New Jersey, and other military bases had been infiltrated by spies and Communists. Even though his subcommittee hearings failed to uncover a single spy or Communist, he did discover an army dentist, Irving Peress, at Camp Kilmer, New Jersey, who on his loyalty forms had cited the Fifth Amendment when he was questioned about communist activities. According to one historian, the dentist "was probably the closest Joseph McCarthy ever came to discovering a communist anywhere." Peress had been inducted into the army in January 1953, and, as a dentist, had been automatically promoted to major the following October. Due to his refusal to answer questions on the loyalty forms, on February 2, 1954 (more than a year after his induction), he was given an honorable discharge.

In his hearings, McCarthy launched a blistering attack on the army, bullying and insulting General Ralph Zwicker, a war hero and the commanding officer at Camp Kilmer. The army had acted slowly on the Peress case, and McCarthy was angered because the dentist had been promoted and discharged honorably.

By publicly humiliating Zwicker, McCarthy threatened the morale and honor of the army itself. Both President Eisenhower, a former army general who had commanded the Allied forces in World War II, and

Instead of refuting his accusations, President Dwight D. Eisenhower (1890-1969), a former five-star general, chose to isolate himself from fellow-Republican McCarthy.

Robert Stevens, the secretary of the army, were infuriated by McCarthy. The army charged him with seeking special treatment for Schine. McCarthy countercharged that the army was using Schine as a hostage to blackmail the senator into dropping his subcommittee investigations.

Knowing that so many Americans were watching, Welch paraded a number of top army men in full uniform into the hearing room to sit near him and Secretary Stevens. He wanted to make it clear that he represented the U.S. Army, not just a few bureaucrats. Their display angered McCarthy. "Point of order, Mr. Chairman," he snapped, wanting to know how so many generals and colonels could spend time at the hearings instead of performing their duties for the army.

McCarthy spent the first 14 days of the hearings baiting Stevens with accusatory questions. Early in the proceedings, however, Welch gained the upper hand by challenging a photograph introduced by subcommittee counsel Ray Jenkins that showed Stevens smiling at Schine. McCarthy had called this photograph evidence that Stevens was being "especially nice" to Schine so that McCarthy would drop his army investigations. Welch showed how the photo had been cropped to make it appear as if Schine and Stevens were alone together. Then he produced the original photograph, which included two other men. He charged that "a doctored or altered photograph" had been produced in the courtroom "as if it were honest."

"Point of order!" cried McCarthy. He accused Welch of lying. Roy Cohn also claimed to know nothing about the original photograph, but soon McCarthy aide James Juliana admitted to cropping the picture.

On May 4, when Secretary Stevens was on the stand, McCarthy introduced a classified letter from the FBI to the army that warned of espionage at Fort Monmouth. Welch countered by asking FBI director J. Edgar Hoover to verify that he had written and mailed the document, but Hoover denied any knowledge of the letter. When it was revealed that the FBI had never followed through on

While Director J. Edgar Hoover (1895-1972) made the Federal Bureau of Investigation a highly efficient weapon against crime, he has also been accused of trampling on the civil rights of innocent people.

the original report because of lack of evidence, Welch, who had suspected that the letter was phony, called it "a carbon copy of precisely nothing." The question that remained was how McCarthy had obtained classified information.

When called to the witness stand, McCarthy refused to answer questions about the letter or how he had acquired it. He said only that an army intelligence officer had given him the document out of "duty to his country." Repeatedly McCarthy evaded Welch's questions on the stand. Roy Cohn later observed that in his refusal to

*Before his appointment as chief counsel to McCarthy's
senate subcommittee, lawyer Roy Cohn (right) had
helped to convict spies Julius and Ethel Rosenberg in
1951 for passing atomic secrets to the Soviets.*

cooperate, McCarthy sounded "like the many dozens of
witnesses he himself had criticized."

Millions saw McCarthy do what he had ridiculed
and condemned so many others for doing—refusing to
answer the questions of a congressional subcommittee.
McCarthy's name for those who had refused to answer
questions by invoking their constitutional rights had been
"Fifth Amendment Communists." Many now wondered
why McCarthy's refusal to answer was any different.

The climactic showdown came on June 9, 1954, several weeks into the hearings. Welch had discovered that McCarthy and Cohn had kept the phony FBI document about Fort Monmouth in their possession for months and had not notified Secretary Stevens of its existence.

"You didn't tug his lapel and say, 'Mr. Secretary, I know something about Monmouth that won't let me sleep nights?'" Welch asked Cohn. Welch then said that he hoped if Cohn knew about Communists in the government, he would warn someone "by sundown. Whenever you learn of them from now on, Mr. Cohn," said Welch, "I beg of you, will you tell somebody about them quick?" Welch was ridiculing Cohn, and McCarthy was furious.

"Point of order!" cried McCarthy. He then turned on Welch, charging that a man in Welch's law firm named Fred Fisher had belonged to the Lawyers Guild, an organization that had represented the Communist Party.

Welch knew about Fisher's past affiliation with the group and for that reason had asked him not to assist in the hearings. In fact, the *New York Times* had printed a story about Welch sending Fisher back to Boston.

Even Roy Cohn sat shaking his head as McCarthy spoke, and Joseph Welch was horrified and angry. When he spoke, his voice shook with emotion. With tears glistening in his eyes, Welch addressed McCarthy:

> Little did I dream you could be so reckless and so cruel as to do an injury to that lad. . . . I fear he shall always bear a scar, needlessly inflicted by you. . . . I like to think I'm a gentleman, but your forgiveness will have to come from someone other than me.

During the Army-McCarthy hearings, McCarthy (right) tried to cast suspicion on evidence and deflect questions from Welch (left).

McCarthy continued to attack Fisher despite Welch's powerful rebuke. "Let us not assassinate this lad further, Senator," Welch cut in. "You have done enough. Have you no sense of decency, sir, at long last? Have you left no sense of decency?"

When once again McCarthy tried to criticize Fisher, Welch interrupted sternly. "I will not discuss this with you further. You have sat within six feet of me and could have asked me about Fred Fisher." Finished with his questioning of Cohn, Welch asked the committee chairman to call his next witness. The room erupted into applause. Even members of the press clapped for Welch.

Chairman Mundt had no choice but to call a recess. McCarthy slouched in his seat, ignored by everyone.

The next day, newspapers all across the country ran pictures of an outraged Joseph Welch. Headlines read, "HAVE YOU NO SENSE OF DECENCY?"

Although the hearings continued until June 17, McCarthy had lost his credibility. The committee concluded that both the army and McCarthy were at fault. Cohn's actions were found improper, and he resigned as committee counsel. Welch declared that if nothing else had been accomplished by the hearings, they had kept McCarthy on television long enough for the public to get a good look at him.

The U.S. Senate voted on December 2, 1954, to condemn McCarthy. Although he remained a senator, the power and influence he had wielded for so many years was gone, and his colleagues avoided him. His health began to fail, and he died on May 2, 1957.

After the Army-McCarthy hearings, Joseph Welch returned to his law practice in Boston. But the American public did not forget his gentle, folksy charm and sharp wit. Until his death on October 6, 1960, Welch received hundreds of fan letters each month.

Writing after the hearings, Welch noted how McCarthy was fond of the accusatory words "Fifth Amendment Communist." "The Fifth Amendment has been resorted to . . . by many rascals, by many guilty men," Welch acknowledged. "But no matter who invokes the amendment, it stands in our Constitution as one of the guardians of our liberties."

Morris Dees, director of the Southern Poverty Law Center, has persevered despite a 1983 arson attack, a 1984 assassination attempt, and continuing death threats from white supremacists.

8

Morris Dees
Fighting Hatred

*R*obert Shelton, the Imperial Wizard of the United Klans of America, sat on the witness stand and held exhibit number 17 in his hands.

"What is this a picture of?" asked Morris Dees, the attorney for Beulah Mae Donald, the plaintiff.

"It's a picture of an individual looking out," Shelton replied. "Apparently, it's a white man." Following Dees's request, he went on to read the words on the picture: "It's terrible the way blacks are being treated. All whites should work to give the blacks what they deserve. Turn page." Shelton turned the page of the 1979 issue of the

Fiery Cross, a Klan publication. The next page revealed a drawing of an obviously dead black man with a rope around his neck, hanging from a tree. Dees pointed to the bottom of the page.

"It says down here 'Robert Shelton, editor and publisher.' Is that right?"

"Yes," answered Shelton.

Dees let the jury members, one by one, examine the publication. The drawing of the black lynching victim clearly shocked some of them.

In March 1981, the body of a 19-year-old black man named Michael Donald was found hanging from a tree in Mobile, Alabama. Dees showed the jury a photograph of Donald's battered body. The similarity between the drawing from the magazine two years earlier and the police photo of Donald's body was obvious.

In February 1987, the civil case of *Beulah Mae Donald v. United Klans of America*, brought by the victim's mother, was being heard in Mobile. Two men were already in prison for the murder of Michael Donald. The first, James "Tiger" Knowles, had confessed to the killing in exchange for a reduced sentence of life in prison. The second, Henry Hays, had received the death penalty. He was the son of Bennie Hays, the second-highest-ranking Klan official in southern Alabama.

There are several Klan groups, but the United Klans of America was the largest and most violent at that time. In 1963, its members had bombed the Birmingham, Alabama, Sixteenth Street Baptist Church, killing four young girls. The United Klans had also terrorized blacks

Robert Shelton founded the United Klans of America in 1961. Since that time, his Klan faction has been implicated in a number of murders and terrorist attacks.

and civil rights workers during the civil rights movement in the 1960s.

Morris Dees, cofounder and executive director of the Southern Poverty Law Center, was convinced that Klansmen other than Knowles and Hays were involved in the murder. He decided to bring a civil suit against the Klan to prove that they were responsible for Donald's death and that Knowles and Hays had acted as representatives of the Klan. When Beulah Mae Donald agreed to sue the United Klans of America, Dees began a two-year investigation of the case, building a chain of evidence that would link the Klan directly to the Donald murder.

Dees became the first attorney to file suit against a racist organization. In doing so, he hoped to make the leaders financially responsible for the violent actions of individuals within the organization. If the jury members ruled in favor of Beulah Mae Donald, their verdict would be a landmark precedent-setting decision.

Born in 1936, Dees learned about inequality at an early age. The Dees family grew cotton on a 110-acre farm in Mount Meigs, Alabama. Although the Dees family was white, they had many black neighbors. Dees credits his father for his commitment to justice. "Daddy gave black people something that was even scarcer than money—respect," Dees remembered. "Just sitting with black friends of my daddy's, I began to feel their hurt, and I took it personal."

The life of a tenant farmer was a hard one, so young Morris was determined to save enough money to buy his own land. He delivered newspapers, sold peaches, and turned in Coke bottles for a penny each. Then he started buying cattle and pigs from his neighbors. "The going price for young pigs weighing up to 80 pounds was five dollars," Dees wrote in his autobiography, *A Season for Justice*. "I'd fatten 'em up to over 210 pounds and then sell them for forty-five dollars." He also raised chickens and sold them to local stores.

By the time Dees graduated from high school in 1955, he had $5,000 in the bank, 50 head of cattle, and 200 hogs. That same year, he entered the University of Alabama as a prelaw major.

When a federal court ordered the university to admit its first black student in 1956, Dees watched as 10,000 angry whites and dozens of Klansmen screamed "Nigger, go home!" at the young black woman. "I felt sick to my stomach," Dees later wrote. "This was the first time I had ever seen Klansmen in action. The first time I had ever seen a mob."

During his college years, Dees started a mail-order business. After his mother sent him a fruitcake for his birthday, Dees wrote to the parents of each student, offering to deliver a freshly baked cake to their child on his or her birthday. The "'Bama Birthday Cake Service" netted over a thousand dollars a month. Dees soon took on Millard Fuller as a partner and expanded into selling fundraising products to clubs and other organizations. During their university years, their sales reached nearly a half-million dollars.

Fuller and Dees then attended the University of Alabama's law school and afterward opened a law practice in Montgomery. They continued their mail-order business and added books to their catalog of items. Their first title, *Favorite Recipes of Home Economics Teachers*, sold 250,000 copies. The business became so successful that the two men closed their law office.

In 1965, Dees and Fuller assisted in the 49-mile Selma-to-Montgomery march led by civil rights leader Martin Luther King Jr. This was the first time that Dees had taken part in a civil rights event. Three years later, after reading Clarence Darrow's 1934 autobiography, *The Story of My Life*, Dees made a decision that changed the course of his life. Dees shared Darrow's sympathies for people who were poor, struggling, and vulnerable, and he admired the fact that Darrow took on cases that "made legal history in the fight for human dignity and justice for the powerless." Realizing how similar Darrow's views were to his own, Dees decided to sell his mail-order business and "specialize in civil rights law." In 1969, he sold the company to Times Mirror for $6 million. (Millard Fuller had left the firm several years earlier to establish what in 1976 became Habitat for Humanity, a non-profit organization that assists low-income families in building their own homes.)

Taking on Joe Levin as his new law partner, Dees began to accept civil rights cases that dealt with such issues as freedom of speech and the rights of women and minorities. They soon founded the Southern Poverty Law Center, which offered free legal service to those who could not afford to pay. The fees from their paying clients and donations from supporters throughout the United

States supported the nonpaying cases. For the first few years, Dees received no pay, but as the center expanded to include a staff of more than 40 people with 5 full-time lawyers, he accepted a salary as the center's executive director.

One of the center's first cases involved the integration of the Montgomery YMCA. When sisters Annie Ruth Smith and Mary Louise Smith attempted to register their seven-year-old sons, Vincent and Edward, in the Y's two-week summer camp program, they were told that the children could not enroll "because it was an all-white camp." The Y's lawyers argued that civil rights laws did not apply because they were a private organization. In *Smith v. YMCA* (1969), Dees claimed that "the YMCA's recreational programs constituted public accommodations," so rejecting the Smith boys because of race violated the Civil Rights Act of 1964. Also, since the Y received government benefits, it was "required . . . to comply with the standards embodied in the Equal Protection Clause of the Fourteenth Amendment."

Eventually, Judge Frank M. Johnson Jr. granted an order prohibiting the YMCA from denying membership to blacks, recruiting at white schools without also recruiting at black schools, and excluding blacks from their boards of directors.

In another early case, Dees and Levin sued the state of Alabama in order to integrate the Alabama state troopers, which in 37 years had never had a black officer. "The all-white force was a symbol of the brutal racism that had gripped Alabama for so long," wrote Dees. Although

Initially formed after the Civil War to fight for white supremacy, the Ku Klux Klan was reorganized in the 1920s and again in the 1960s to persecute ethnic and religious minorities, including blacks, immigrants, Catholics, and Jews.

they won the case in a federal district court in 1972, the issue was not settled until 1987 when the U.S. Supreme Court upheld the lower court's decision.

By the late 1970s, the strength and visibility of the Ku Klux Klan had increased throughout the United States. To combat its growth, Dees set up "Klanwatch" to monitor Klan events and activities and bring suit against those who violated the civil rights of others. In the Gulf

140

Coast port of Seabrook, Texas, in 1981, tension grew between white American fishermen and fishermen who had recently immigrated from Vietnam. The Klan harassed and threatened the Vietnamese, destroying their boats and burning crosses in their yards. The Klansman in charge was Louis Beam, the Grand Dragon of the Texas Knights of the Ku Klux Klan. "I've got the Bible in one hand and a thirty-eight in the other hand," Beam once said at a Klan convention, "and I know what to do."

Dees and the Southern Poverty Law Center filed suit in federal court for an injunction against Klan members on behalf of Nguyen Van Nam and the Vietnamese Fishermen's Association. During the trial, Dees requested a court order prohibiting the Klan and other Americans from interfering with the immigrants' rights to fish. The judge ruled against the Klan and barred them from acts of violence and intimidation. This was the first of several confrontations between the Klan and Morris Dees. He received numerous death threats, and the police arrested armed would-be assassins on his property on three different occasions. Following those incidents, Dees traveled with armed bodyguards and often carried a gun for protection.

On July 21, 1983, using stationery of the Aryan Nations, a white supremacist group, Louis Beam wrote to Dees that they should go out into the woods "and settle once and for all the enmity that exists between us. Two go in—one comes out." One week later, the Southern Poverty Law Center was badly damaged by arsonists. An editorial in the *White Patriot*, a monthly publication of the

*On July 28, 1983, members of the Ku Klux Klan
tried to burn down the Southern Poverty Law Center,
but the careful storage of documents at the center and
the arsonists' lack of skill saved the center's work.*

Alabama Ku Klux Klan, suggested that the fire was "an Act of God" in retribution for the harassment of the Klan by the center's attorneys.

Instead of curtailing his activities, Dees wrote that "the torching of the Center had made my battle against the Klan personal as well as philosophical." In late 1984, three men were arrested and convicted of starting the fire. Tommy Downs and Charles Bailey had been hired by Klansman Joe Garner to burn the building because he was "tired of Dees aggravating the hell out of me and all the harassment, depositions, and subpoenas."

It was also in 1984 that Henry Hays went on trial for the murder of Michael Donald. Tiger Knowles, who had confessed to the killing, testified against Hays. "Henry Hays and I abducted Michael Donald on Friday night in the latter part of March 1981," Knowles explained. The two "took him to Baldwin County where he was beaten and strangled to death and later on early that Saturday morning he was hanged from this tree on Herndon Avenue." Both Knowles and Hays were Klan members and had murdered Donald "simply because he was black in order to show the strength of the Klan, . . . to show that they were still here in Alabama."

When Knowles linked the Klan to the murder, Dees began to plan a civil suit against them. He filed his landmark case, *Beulah Mae Donald v. United Klans of America*, in 1987, six years after the Donald lynching. During the course of the trial, Dees traced the Klan's history of violence from the 1960s. Then he called convicted murderer Tiger Knowles to the stand.

Dees showed Knowles the drawing of the lynched black man in the *Fiery Cross* and asked whether the picture had influenced him to hang a black person. Knowles replied, "This was a publication of the Klan telling us what we should do and telling the Klan's beliefs; that's what we should do, go out and hang black people."

In his closing argument, 51-year-old Dees addressed the jury members: "You will have an opportunity to send a . . . message" that would "ring out from the top" of the courthouse and "be heard all over Alabama and all over the United States: That an all-white jury from the heart of the South . . . [would no longer] tolerate racial violence in any way, shape, or form." Although no amount of money could ever truly compensate Beulah Mae Donald for the loss of her son, Dees told the jury, if they returned "a large verdict—a very large verdict," they would be telling Beulah Mae Donald that "her son's life was as valuable and as precious as anyone's."

After four and one-half hours of deliberation, the jury ruled for the plaintiff and against the United Klans of America and awarded damages of $7 million. "History will show," wrote Morris Dees, "that an all-white Southern jury had held the Klan accountable."

Since the United Klans of America had no major assets, they were forced to turn over to Beulah Mae Donald their new headquarters—a 7,400-square-foot building in Tuscaloosa, Alabama. She sold the building for $55,000 and moved from public housing into her first home. Less than a year later, Donald died of a heart condition. But her suit had bankrupted the Klan.

At the close of the trial, James "Tiger" Knowles apologized to Beulah Mae Donald (shown with Dees) for killing her son. She sat motionless and then replied softly, "I forgive you."

By now, Dees and the Southern Poverty Law Center were also battling new extremist groups. The White Aryan Resistance and White Pride members were rebellious young men. They shaved their heads—earning for themselves the name "skinheads"—and wore black leather clothing and combat boots. The members of these neo-Nazi organizations admired dictator Adolf Hitler and the policies of Hitler's Third Reich in Germany, and they advocated violence against minorities.

On November 13, 1988, Mulugeta Seraw, a 28-year-old Ethiopian, was murdered in Portland, Oregon. The police arrested three skinheads—members of the East Side White Pride gang—who pleaded guilty to the crime.

Over 1,000 miles away, in Fallbrook, California, Tom Metzger, the 50-year-old leader of the White Aryan Resistance (WAR), announced the murder on his nationwide telephone hotline. "Sounds like the skinheads did a civic duty," he declared.

Dees and the Southern Poverty Law Center staff began to accumulate evidence to build a case showing a direct link between Metzger's philosophy of racial violence and the murder of Mulugeta Seraw. Just as he had done in *Beulah Mae Donald v. United Klans of America*, Dees filed a suit, this time against Metzger and his organization to hold them financially accountable for Seraw's murder.

On September 17, 1990, Dees received an anonymous letter in which he was told that "there could be very bad things happen to you if you carry out this exercise in futility [suing Tom Metzger]." The letter warned, "You are taking on too much, Morris baby, you are messing with white power. Nobody messes with white power. You go against nature."

The trial began in Portland on October 10, 1990. Under Oregon law, only 9 of the 12 jurors needed to decide for one side in civil cases. Tom Metzger had good lawyers but chose to represent himself in the trial. He was a smooth talker and had been on many television talk shows. He did not believe he could lose.

Dave Mazzella, a former WAR youth division vice-president, had agreed to testify against the leader of the

146

White Aryan Resistance. Mazzella had been very close to Metzger, who was like "a second father" to him. "I was willing to die for him and his beliefs and for WAR," recalled Mazzella.

On the stand, 21-year-old Mazzella admitted that Tom Metzger and his son, John, had instructed him to teach skinhead recruits to commit violent acts against minorities and had sent him to Portland in 1988 to organize East Side White Pride. "Skinheads will only respect someone who is violent," Mazzella explained to the jury.

When Dees asked Mazzella why he had come forward to testify, he answered, "I didn't feel right about everything I have done in my life. I did a lot of bad things, a lot of evil things, and I wanted to come clean."

In his closing argument, Dees declared that the case was "important for the community, for the state, for the nation." He told the jury that its verdict would have "far-reaching effects" and that he hoped it would tell "Tom Metzger and his organization and all other people who peddle and preach hate and violence" that a jury in Oregon had said, "No. We are going to stop you right here." If they returned a verdict of $12.5 million for the family of Mulugeta Seraw, Dees told the jury, "the case would make history."

Nearly five hours later, the jury reached its verdict. By a vote of 11 to 1, they found Tom Metzger and his White Aryan Resistance guilty on all counts. They decided to award Seraw's family $2.5 million in damages for Mulugeta Seraw's pain, suffering, and unrealized future earnings and $10 million in punitive damages.

After the verdict was announced, Metzger held a press conference. "The movement will not be stopped in the puny town of Portland," he declared. "We're in your colleges, we're in your armies, we're in your police forces. . . . Where do you think . . . these skinheads disappeared to?"

To enforce the judgment, the court ordered the sale of Metzger's home and personal property and made provisions to *garnish*, or take a portion of, his wages for the next 20 years. The court also prohibited him from engaging in white supremacist activities for three years.

Following the 1990 Metzger trial, the Southern Poverty Law Center began a new project, "Teaching Tolerance." In the following years, they have distributed free teaching kits and a biannual magazine to more than 500,000 U.S. teachers to help them explore racial and ethnic tolerance with their students.

Morris Dees remains vigilant against racial violence in the face of continued threats, including a 1995 plot by an Oklahoma militia group to blow up the Southern Poverty Law Center. The center's new headquarters in Montgomery, built as a monument to justice, houses a memorial that lists the names of 40 men, women, and children who were killed during the civil rights movement in the 1960s. The words of Martin Luther King Jr. that are engraved on the black granite monument sum up the life and philosophy of attorney Morris Dees: "We will not be satisfied until justice rolls down like waters and righteousness like a mighty stream."

Bibliography

Aymar, Brandt, and Edward Sagarin. *Laws and Trials that Created History*. New York: Crown, 1974.

Barton, William E. *The Life of Abraham Lincoln*. Vol. I. Indianapolis: Bobbs-Merrill, 1925.

Berson, Robin Kadison. *Marching to a Different Drummer: Unrecognized Heroes of American History*. Westport, CT: Greenwood, 1994.

Bowen, Catherine Drinker. *John Adams and the American Revolution*. New York: Grosset & Dunlap, 1949.

Boynick, David K. *Women Who Led the Way: Eight Pioneers for Equal Rights*. New York: Thomas Y. Crowell, 1959.

Brown, Drollene P. *Belva Lockwood Wins Her Case*. Niles, IL: Albert Whitman, 1987.

Cohn, Roy. *McCarthy*. New York: New American Library, 1968.

Cook, Fred J. *The Army-McCarthy Hearings*. New York: Franklin Watts, 1971.

David, Andrew. *Famous Criminal Trials*. Minneapolis: Lerner, 1979.

Dees, Morris, with Steve Fiffer. *A Season for Justice: The Life and Times of Civil Rights Lawyer Morris Dees*. New York: Charles Scribner's Sons, 1991.

———. *Hate on Trial: The Case against America's Most Dangerous Neo-Nazi*. New York: Villard Books, 1993.

Duff, John J. *A. Lincoln—Prairie Lawyer*. New York: Rinehart, 1960.

Ewald, William Bragg, Jr. *Who Killed Joe McCarthy?* New York: Simon & Schuster, 1984.

Ferling, John E. *John Adams, A Life*. Knoxville: University of Tennessee Press, 1992.

Fisher, Joshua Francis. "Andrew Hamilton, Esq., of Pennsylvania," *Pennsylvania Magazine of History and Biography* 16 (1892): 1-27.

Fox, Mary Virginia. *Lady for the Defense: A Biography of Belva Lockwood*. New York: Harcourt Brace Jovanovich, 1975.

Frank, John P. *Lincoln As a Lawyer*. Urbana: University of Illinois Press, 1961.

Freedman, Russell. *Lincoln: A Photobiography*. New York: Clarion Books, 1987.

Friedman, Leon, and Fred L. Israel, eds. *The Justices of the United States Supreme Court*, Vol. 4. New York: Chelsea House, 1969.

Gerhart, Eugene C. *America's Advocate: Robert H. Jackson*. Indianapolis: Bobbs-Merrill, 1958.

Havemann, Ernest. "The Men McCarthy Made Famous," *Life* 36, no. 20 (May 17, 1954): 47-56.

Hertz, Emanuel. *The Hidden Lincoln: From the Letters and Papers of William H. Herndon*. New York: Viking, 1938.

Hill, Frederick Trevor. *Lincoln the Lawyer*. New York: Century, 1906.

Jackson, Joseph. "Who Was Andrew Hamilton?" *Pennsylvania Magazine of History and Biography* 56 (1932): 275-277.

Jackson, Robert H. *The Nürnberg Case*. New York: Alfred A. Knopf, 1947.

Kilmuir, Lord Viscount. "Justice Jackson and Nuremberg: A British Tribute," *Stanford Law Review* 8 (December 1955): 54-59.

Konkle, Burton Alva. *The Life of Andrew Hamilton, 1676-1741*. Philadelphia: National, 1941.

Kornstein, Daniel J. *Thinking Under Fire: Great Courtroom Lawyers and Their Impact on American History*. New York: Dodd, Mead, 1987.

Kunhardt, Philip B., Jr., Philip B. Kunhardt III, and Peter W. Kunhardt. *Lincoln: An Illustrated Biography*. New York: Alfred A. Knopf, 1992.

Latham, Frank B. *The Trial of John Peter Zenger, August 1735: An Early Fight for America's Freedom of the Press*. New York: Franklin Watts, 1970.

Miller, Helen Hill. *The Case for Liberty*. Chapel Hill: University of North Carolina Press, 1965.

Newsweek, "That Sly Counselor—Welch," 18, no. 23 (June 7, 1954): 27-31.

Persico, Joseph E. *Nuremberg: Infamy on Trial*. New York: Viking, 1994.

Reeves, Thomas C. *The Life and Times of Joe McCarthy*. New York: Stein & Day, 1982.

Rutherfurd, Livingston. *John Peter Zenger*. New York: Dodd, Mead, 1904.

Sandburg, Carl. *Abraham Lincoln: The Prairie Years and The War Years*. Norwalk, CT: Easton, 1954.

Settle, Mary Lee. *The Scopes Trial: The State of Tennessee v. John Thomas Scopes*. New York: Schulte, 1963.

Sheperd, Jack. *The Adams Chronicles*. Boston: Little, Brown, 1975.

Smith, Page. *John Adams*. 2 vols. Garden City, NY: Doubleday, 1962.

Stern, Madeleine B. *We the Women: Career Firsts of Nineteenth-Century America*. New York: Schulte, 1963.

Stone, Irving. *Clarence Darrow for the Defense*. Garden City, NY: Doubleday, 1941.

Taylor, Telford. *The Anatomy of the Nuremberg Trials: A Personal Memoir*. New York: Alfred A. Knopf, 1992.

Urofsky, Melvin I., ed. *The Supreme Court Justices: A Biographical Dictionary*. New York: Garland, 1994.

Weinberg, Arthur, and Lila Weinberg. *Clarence Darrow: A Sentimental Rebel*. New York: Atheneum, 1987.

Welch, Joseph N. "The Lawyer's Afterthoughts," *Life* 37, no. 4 (July 26, 1954): 96-108.

Woldman, Albert A. *Lawyer Lincoln*. Boston: Houghton Mifflin, 1936.

Woodward, Grace Steele. *The Cherokees*. Norman: University of Oklahoma Press, 1963.

Zobel, Hiller B. *The Boston Massacre*. New York: W.W. Norton, 1970.

Index

159

ABOUT THE AUTHOR

PHYLLIS RAYBIN EMERT has written more than 30 books for young readers on a wide variety of topics, including sports and athletes, airplanes, automobiles, and unsolved mysteries. Some of her recent titles include *Women in the Civil War: Warriors, Patriots, Nurses, and Spies*; *Colonial Triangular Trade: An Economy Based on Human Misery*; and *True Valor: Real Stories of Brave Men and Women in World War II*. Emert, who has a master's degree in political science, lives in southern California with her husband and their two children.

Photo Credits